Copyright © 2023 Klaus Krippendorff
All rights reserved
ISBN - 978-1-7372531-2-9
Cover design: E-Rose Creative

Klaus: A Memoir

Klaus Krippendorff

Table of Contents

Krippendorff Family Tree

Section 1: Family History and Early Childhood   01

Section 2: From Halberstadt to Ratingen   15

Section 3: Ulm, Princeton, and coming to Philadelphia   49

Section 4: Marriage and Children   67

Section 5: Career   86

Conclusion   103

"Metaphor: A Better Picture of the World"   112

Klaus's CV   114

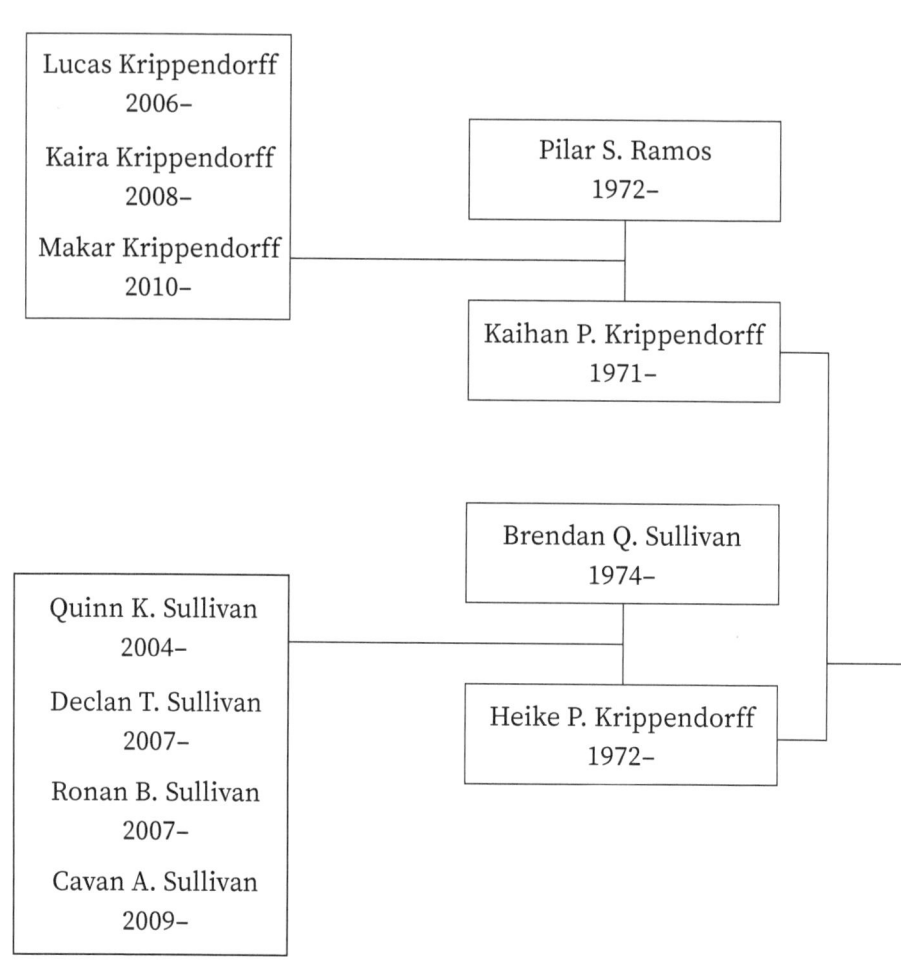

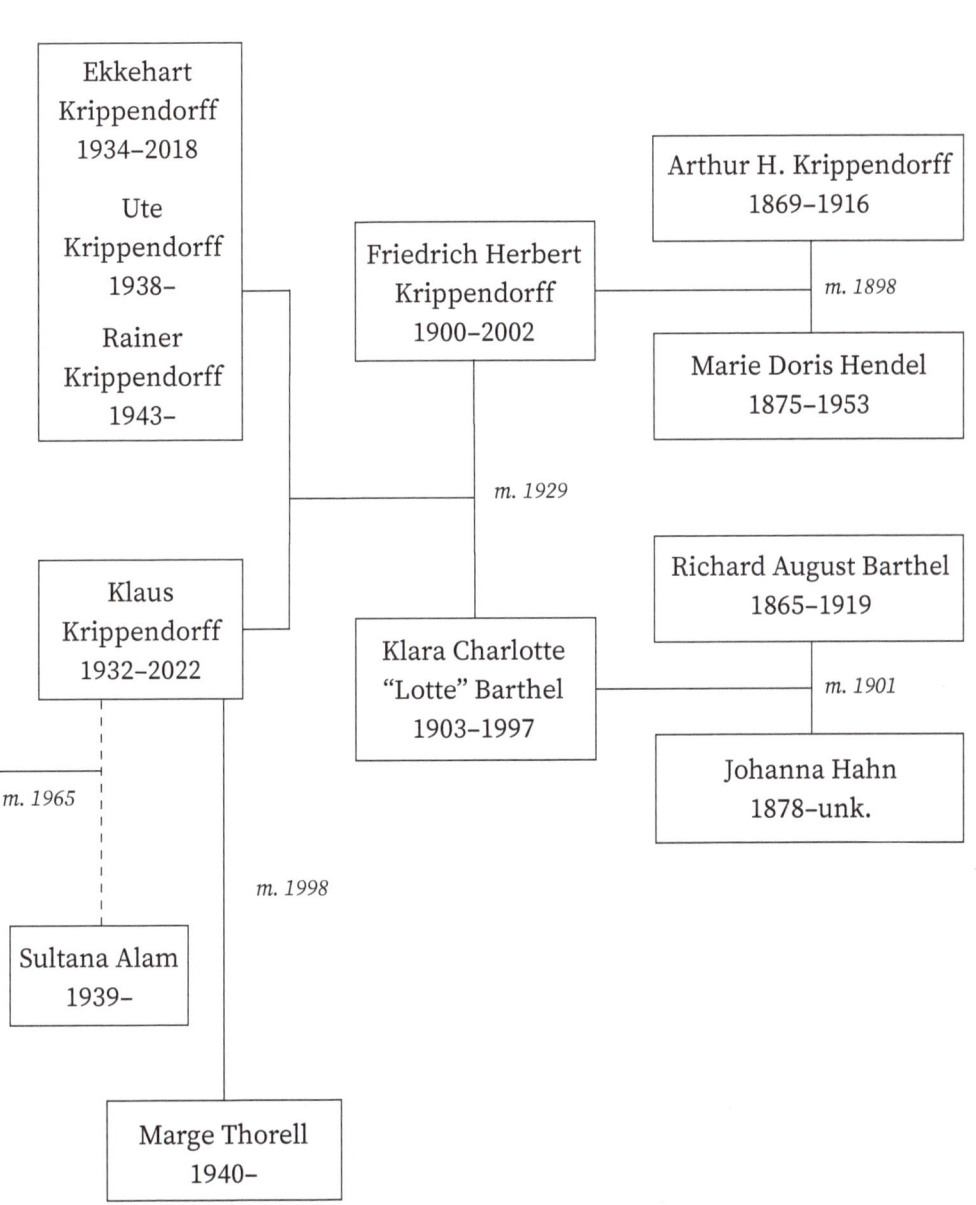

Krippendorff Family Tree

Introduction

What follows is the life story of our father, Klaus Krippendorff, as told by Klaus himself. He had a fascinating life, from growing up in Germany during World War II to experiencing the unique educational opportunities offered at *Hochschule für Gestaltung* in Ulm, then coming to America to undertake pioneering work in content analysis, cybernetics, and design. His academic influence was vast, with over 250 publications, all while serving as the longest-tenured faculty member in the history of the University of Pennsylvania. His work will long outlast him. As his wife, Marge Thorell, said, "He could hear the dog-whistle that no one else could." We encourage anyone interested in learning more about his academic work to refer to the full bibliography of his published materials at the end of this book. Of particular interest might be the article he wrote in 2008, "Designing in Ulm and Off Ulm," about that very particular place and time in history. "Undoing Power," published in 1995, is also a seminal and much-heralded piece that gives the reader a sense of Klaus's style and focus.

Klaus was also our *papa*. We're the ones who encouraged him to write about his life so we could capture his thoughts and recollections before they were lost. As with any memoir, this one draws from Klaus's memory. There will naturally be differences in how others may remember things, and there are indeed discrepancies with Klaus's mother's memoir. He wrote this book in what would be the last year of his life and passed away before he could produce the closing chapter about his retirement years, his fulfilling marriage with Marge, and the pleasure he took in being a grandfather. Nor did he have a chance to review the manuscript, refine his thoughts, or even check for errors and omissions. We, along with Marge, stepped in to add what we could, and have incorporated our own memories of Klaus's second marriage, continued work, and time with grandchildren, which made his last few decades so meaningful.

Kaihan P. Krippendorff
Heike Krippendorff Sullivan

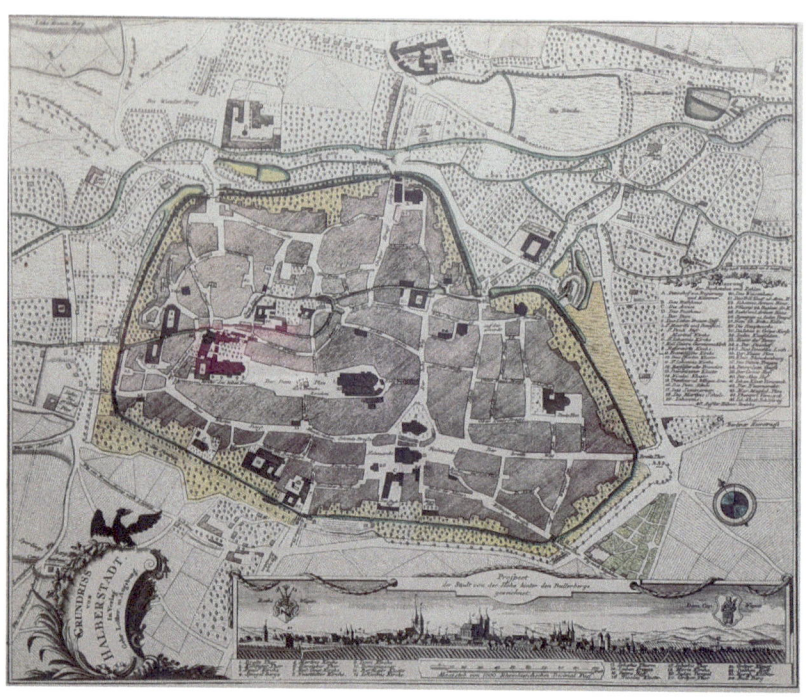

Map of Halberstadt

Section 1
Family History and Early Childhood

The Krippendorffs and Herbert Krippendorff

Much of the family history we have access to is from the research done by my grandfather, Arthur Heinrich Krippendorff (1859–1916), whom I never met. When he was young, he went from church to church to find wedding, birth, and death records. He is the one who uncovered the Krippendorff family history, but he just looked for Krippendorffs, he did not research the wives' families.

The stories I know start with my great-great-grandfather, Ernst Heinrich Krippendorff (known as Heinrich; 1780–1859), who served the King of Saxony as ambassador in Hamburg. Heinrich lived in Dresden during the time of the Napoleonic Wars, and he was probably what we'd call a mover and shaker today. During the French occupation of Dresden in 1813, they demanded that Dresden provide horses for the military. He knew enough people to manage to get some horses for the French and had a role in saving Dresden. Later, when Russian soldiers occupied Dresden, Heinrich was attacked by five Russian soldiers while he was taking a walk. He had a walking stick with him that had a lead ball on top. With that he defended himself. After chasing the Russians away, he continued walking and a woman ran up to him saying there were other Russians trying to rape someone just further down the road. He went to help and was able to defend this woman. In Dresden he was in charge of a bridge, and I was told that he got into difficulty with the city about the collection of bridge tolls. Dresden is on the Elbe River, one of the main rivers in Europe, which runs from the Czech Republic to Hamburg. His job was to ensure money was collected from everyone who crossed the bridge. At some point a city representative wanted to cross the bridge without paying the fee. Heinrich didn't allow that and was fired, though he was later reinstated in this role.

Going farther back, other Krippendorffs include a physician, a priest who was a military chaplain, tanners, and an organ builder. The farthest back Arthur got in his research was Georg Krippendörffer (1549–1611), who was a magistrate in Efurt, which is a relatively big city in the German state of Thuringia, between Dresden and Frankfurt.

What my grandfather didn't know or at least didn't mention is that there is a tiny little village called Krippendorf, in Thuringia in east-central Germany, between Saxony and Bavaria. Marge and I visited that village; it had maybe 200 inhabitants. I can't say exactly when it was founded but it was a long time ago, maybe 1,000 years ago, by a farmer named Creppen or Greppen; the spelling was never clear. In the church of this little village, we saw a stone used for baptisms that is engraved with the name Greppendorf.

I spent a little time researching the history of the town and found that in the 1400s, the ruler of the area erased this village from the map. There's a German word, *schleifen,* that means making flat, to raze. That's what happened to this village and the neighboring village. I have been struggling to find out why,

The Krippendorff Family Crest

and I've not found a single reason. It could be that the townspeople were very disobedient, that they didn't pay taxes, or they insulted the ruler. Who knows? Anyway, the village was razed. Shortly afterward, several Krippendorffers appeared in Thuringia. Krippendorffer is the possessive form of the word, with a second "f" as part of the possessive form. So those Krippendorffers, I hypothesize, were the refugees who left the town of Greppendorf. *Krippe* means cradle or crib in German, but that is not the origin of the name of this village.

My grandfather Arthur was a city representative and a lawyer in the small town where my father was born, in the Reichenbach region. When not reelected to his post there, he moved to Dresden, where he opened a law practice. He was actually an academic who studied the law, so he was pretty educated. When he was fifty-five, the First World War started. He was drafted and made an officer because of his status as a highly educated academic. But as an officer he had to ride a horse, which he didn't really know how to do since he was an academic. This next bit may just be a rumor: We know for sure that he died in 1916 in a military hospital due to an operation, but the rumor is that he fell from his horse, got a hernia, and didn't survive.

My father, Friedrich Julius Herbert, known as Herbert, was sixteen when his father died. The post-war years were very hard for my father. Post-WWI Germany was known for a period of hyperinflation in which the German currency lost almost all value. My father and his sister Hilde had to find jobs because the minimal pension my grandmother received was not enough to live on. It was a tough childhood.

I don't know how he worked and went to school at the same time, but he was a student at a technical university from 1920 to 1924 and received a degree in engineering. Part of that education was hands on, so he found a job as a ship's engineer and went to India in 1922. He went all the way to Karachi and back. The story is that he brought back two sacks of rice with him for his mother.

The next part of his hands-on training took him to the United States in 1924. He got a job as a toolmaker, even though he didn't know how to make tools. He told me that in order to get hired he had to show tools he made as a sample. He didn't have any, so he went to a secondhand store and bought tools to get the job, which he did. After a while the boss said to him, "I know you're not a toolmaker, but you're good enough, I'll keep you." More importantly, from there my father went to Detroit to work on the Ford assembly line. At the time, these assembly lines were really just an American thing that didn't exist anywhere else. His knowledge of assembly lines and mass production were fundamental to much of his later success.

After being in the U.S. for about a year, my father went back to Dresden. The next job he was offered took him back to America, to New York, where he managed the German students who came to study and work like he had. It was during this time, from 1926 to 1928, that he arranged the sponsorship for my mother to come to America. (My parents knew each other before they were in love and got married. My mother had been engaged to someone before my father, but her fiancé died in an accident.)

There were two objects my father kept as a souvenir from those days. He hid them in the drawer of his bedroom dresser when I was a boy. One was an American flag with forty-eight stars and the other was a white ball that he had played with in the Suez Canal.

The Barthels and Charlotte (Lotte) Barthel

The Barthel family was well established in Dresden and composed of businesspeople; they had money. My great-grandfather had a very successful hat shop that one of his sons took over. Another of my mother's uncles was a stationer and married a very rich woman. There is a photo of them all in a car that one of them owned—a real luxury at the time. My mother's father, Richard, was the only one who did not go into business. He was a talented artist, a painter. He earned a living through commercial painting but never made much money. Richard and my grandmother Johanna Hahn were married in 1901. The story of how they met is written in my mother's memoirs.

Richard and Johanna loved each other deeply but they were a little separated from the rest of the family because they were comparatively poor. The Barthel brothers frequently helped them financially, which supported the privileged lifestyle in which my mother and her older sister Dorle grew up.

Many elements of my mother's young life were part of a totally different world than what we know today. For instance, the Saxon princesses would come to the family hat shop once a year to buy their hats. The hat shop Barthels didn't have any children, so my mother and Dorle would go stand in line and receive the princesses when they visited the store. The Elbe River freezes over in the winter and so do the lakes nearby. Ice skating was one of the fashionable things to do and my mother knew how. One day the king's entourage, along with a prince, skated by and they somehow bumped into my mother and she fell. The prince came back, helped her up, and asked her if she was okay. She was and said so. But for the next three days, she didn't wash her hands because she had shaken hands with the prince!

The first great tragedy of my mother's life was when her father died in 1919 from the flu. She said his death was really caused from being weakened by the lack of food and other hardships related to the Great War. She was just sixteen years old when he died. She had a very tight bond with him and it was one of the biggest losses of my mother's life—she said so all the time.

His death was a big problem for the whole family. Dorle was a few years older than my mother and was already married, so she was out of the house. (She married a fabric salesman whom I met many times.) My mother had to find a job to earn some money. One of her aunts' husbands hired her as a bookkeeper. She was not really trained for that, but she found out later that the reason she was hired was that the previous bookkeeper was a crook. Then she moved to a bank and worked as a bank employee. I don't know how long she worked there, but after that she became a bookkeeper and organizer of a student housing project for the technical university in Dresden. She was quite beautiful, and I can imagine that she was a star among the male students there.

The Barthels suffered from the effects of hyperinflation the way the Krippendorffs did. It was a terrible time and tragedy struck again in my mother's life: her grandmother on the Hahn side (her mother's mother) killed herself by putting her head in the oven to eliminate what she felt was the pressure of having an extra person in the family to feed and house.

By 1927/1928, my mother saw that many of the students she knew through her job went to the United States for a year. She found the idea of going to America very appealing. She had had a teacher who once told her about the United States, and my mother had dreamed of visiting since then. She found a sponsor and kept asking her mother and stepfather's permission. They finally agreed. Her stepfather got her a wedding band with "Lotte U.S.A. 1928" engraved on it, so people would think she was married. My father, who was still just an acquaintance, helped her get the necessary papers to make the trip. In America, she worked in people's homes as an au pair and a cook, and did other general household duties.

My mother was an early feminist and was ahead of her time in many ways. The trip to America was very unusual—a single, young woman of twenty-five from a good family going to do something like that was a little unheard of. But why not? My mother risked a lot to do that, and she succeeded.

In the United States, she worked in various households. She told me many stories about her time there. She didn't know how to cook and at some point a family asked her to cook spinach. Spinach does not take long to cook, but she cooked it for a long time. The American family looked at the overcooked spinach and asked what it was. "That's the way we eat it," was her quick reply. Another of the stories is seeing Fitzmaurice, Köhl, and von Hühnfeld (the first men to fly nonstop across the Atlantic) in Lakehurst in 1928.

She goes into more detail about her time in America in her memoirs, but these were the kinds of special moments in her memory. More important is something that happened toward the end of her trip. She made friends with some other young Germans and they wanted to make a cross-country trip by car. They suggested that she cook and they would drive. My mother wanted to drive her share, but she didn't know how. She wanted to learn. Her friends showed her the basics on a small patch of road, but one day she asked a taxi driver if he would let her drive his car. He did, and so she felt she was ready to drive across the United States. She had adventures on the trip, including a bear ripping a piece of her coat off in Yellowstone, but they made it back safely. Before returning to Germany, she got engaged to my father at Niagara Falls. Many years later Marge and I went to Niagara Falls. We sailed on a ship called *The Maid of the Mist* and went under the falls. I decided to call my mother and tell her we were there and what ship we were on. She said it was the same ship she and my father took. It was quite fascinating. My parents were married when they returned to Germany in 1929.

She was an extraordinary woman. She was a real "do-er". She was the one who found us places to live and arranged the moves. She had the energy; she was the mover and shaker. This is a minor thing, but she wanted a modern kitchen. What does that mean, modern? Well, we had a garbage disposal. Nobody else had that back then, but she had learned about them and found one for her kitchen. She also went to the Olympics in 1936 in Berlin and always told us the story of seeing Jesse Owens. It was a more historic event than she could have guessed, but it's another example of her wanting to do something and making it happen.

She was a very caring person in every respect, but I think the few lines of poetry that she chose as the opening of her memoir summarize the driving force behind her personality very well:

> *I slept and dreamt that life was joy. I awoke and saw that life was service. I acted and behold, service was joy.*
> —Rabindranath Tagore

Early Years (Rostock)

My parents really cared for each other; they called each other "darling" in English. They were very close and our family was close, too. I had three siblings, Ekkehart (1934–2018), Ute (b. 1938), and Rainer (b. 1943). I was born in Frankfurt, but my early childhood years were spent in Rostock. I played the most with Ekkehart when we were little as he was the closest in age. Unfortunately, there was a very strange parenting philosophy in Germany that encouraged parents to have their children compete with each other. I would never subscribe to that, but it was a dominant way of thinking about

Section 1: Family History and Early Childhood

children and punishment. I know that I often felt unjustly blamed when we fought over toys because I was the older child. I was told I had to be wiser. It didn't mean my mother cared for me less, but it impacted my relationship with Ekkehart.

We were also close with other family members and spent fun times with my mother's family. The second husband of my Barthel grandmother was a brick manufacturer. He had a lot of money and had a house in *Sächsische Schweiz* (Saxony Switzerland)—*Sonneck Haus,* it was called. We went there many, many times. My grandmother was a very warm woman, always laughing. There was a tank on the top of the house for running water, but you had to pump the water up into the tank with a huge wheel located in a shed outside. They had an owl that they kept in a cage. We loved going there. That house was family.

We played games together. One game was a sort of board game that was so primitive it's laughable. We took corks from wine bottles and tied a string on them. The corks would all be put in the middle of a circle, with us all around. Then, you rolled the dice. When a certain number came up you had to catch as many corks as you could. Or you could also pull the corks away by the string. If you pulled a cork too early, then you got a negative point. This is one of the things that we did. Everybody was around the table, both the adults and the children. It was a lot of fun.

We also had summer vacation time in the Harz mountains. My mother collected mushrooms there and we all climbed the Brocken, the highest mountain in Germany. There happened to be a farm near us there and I made friends with one of the boys who took care of the cows. One day I went with him to spend the day walking the cows to the fields. It was a very outdoors childhood, both in the mountains and in town.

On Sunday mornings at home, we often got in my parents' bed and there they told us stories. Bedtime was different than what it is in America. My parents didn't read to us at bedtime before we went to sleep. They did read to us, though, but before dinner. It wasn't to one individual child, but all of us together. Dinner time was for talking. We talked a lot at dinner; it was a time for important conversation. We reported what we had done that day or what news we had received in the mail from family members and friends.

My father was very good with his hands and made toys for us. Woodworking was one of his hobbies. He made jigsaw puzzles by gluing maps to a large piece of plywood and then he would cut out puzzle pieces. He was very crafty and creative. I remember his preparation for the birth announcement for my little sister. He took a

Klaus and Ekkehart holding Ute's homemade birth announcement

photograph of my brother Ekkehart and me, at three and five years old, holding a large painting between us that was covered with a white sheet. He could later write the birth announcement on it. He also made things out of metal. I have four bookends he made. As a family we also painted Easter eggs in the tradition of Ukraine.

Something very strange in my childhood, which I never understood or asked my mother about, was that I had a doll that I loved very much. It was a Black doll. I had a little knapsack for it, and I always had the knapsack set up so the doll could look out. There were no Black people in Germany at that time. I have no idea where it came from or what their motivation was for giving it to me. It maybe had to do with their experience in the United States, but I don't know. It was revolutionary, from the point of view of Germans, to have this Black doll.

Another kind of vacation we took was to the beach at Warnemünde, a short train ride away from Rostock. In the summer we rented one of these little beach huts that gave you shade and a place to store your things. We went there frequently. There were loudspeakers on the beach. I remember the day in 1939 when the voice on the loudspeaker came on and told everyone that England had declared war against Germany. Mother was so upset that we had to pack everything up and go home immediately. I didn't know the implications of war. I don't know if my mother thought the British were about to invade Germany. The idea that they would invade from the Baltic Sea was impossible,

Section 1: Family History and Early Childhood

but she was very upset. We left so quickly that we had to leave our toys and everything else there.

School

I liked school as a child. I started school in Rostock and I admired my teacher, whose name was Buch. I went there for two or three years. One very sad thing that happened was that one of my best friends died of cancer or of some other disease. That was a big loss. I didn't really understand it and it was a big, big shock.

There is not much else to say about school when I was little except for one incident. When I was in kindergarten, my mother bitterly complained about a very long Christian prayer I had learned by heart

Klaus, unk., Ekkehart

at school. Sadly, I don't remember it today, but my mother went to the school and told them this was not what they should teach. She was objecting, I think, to having been drilled to memorize something that I didn't even understand. She may also have been objecting to religious material, I don't know. I was not religiously educated in any way. It wasn't until I was fourteen years old and living with my father's sister Hilde in Dresden that I had to go to a church for confirmation. This is where I heard stories about Christ for the first time. I don't know if my parents would have had me confirmed had I not been living with Tante Hilde.

Childhood Reading

There's a famous German children's book called *Struwwelpeter*. It's a book on how to teach children to be good through examples of very bad children. By the time of the Nazis, it was popular because it showed what "good" little German children should do. One bad little boy caught flies and tore their wings off. He killed birds and hurt dogs. The stories were brutal. In one of the stories, a girl plays with fire and burns to death. All that is left are her shoes. In another, a child loses a finger when playing with scissors. One child never looked in front of him when he walked and of course fell in the water. It goes on and on. One of the most interesting stories is about a little Black boy. I don't know why there was a Black boy in the story since there were no Blacks when I was little and this book was published almost one hundred years before I was born. But the other boys make fun of the Black boy. Then along comes Nicholas (he had roles other than at Christmastime) and he takes the mean boys and dips them in ink so they are black all over. It's an anti-racism story. Another somewhat similar book was about Max and Moritz and the seven wicked pranks these boys did. They end up dead at the end. As a child, I also read the stories of Baron Munchausen.

When I was a boy, my favorite books were by a famous German author, Karl May, who wrote fantastic fiction about American Indians and white explorers. There were heroes and villains, all of them exciting, and they populated our minds. In our younger years, we often put feathers on our heads and played out various adventures we dreamed up from these books. Karl May had never been to the United States, but his stories were wonderful. Much later, my first wife and I went on a camping trip in Canada and there was an Indian reservation close by. My thought was that they should open up a summer resort to teach Indian skills. I mentioned this to a Canadian person whose response was, "Who would ever go?" That is a fundamental difference in attitude. In Germany, American Indians are definitely heroes. Here they are looked down upon. It's really a shame.

These books were all part of my life before we went to Halberstadt and before the war started. After the war started, it was all different. In the Jungvolk, we were given a little booklet every week about the heroism of soldiers and other patriotic things.

Father's Work

My father was an engineer and was highly desirable to German companies because of his experience in America learning about the modern management of factories and his experience in managing

Section 1: Family History and Early Childhood

production. In Rostock, he was in charge of transportation for an airplane factory hangar. I remember at some point during a very cold winter a water line on the way between the city of Rostock and his factory broke and created a very thick layer of ice on top of the street. No traffic could get through and my father was the one who had to handle that situation. That must have been 1939 or before 1940. At some point he was sent to Poland after the Germans invaded to organize a factory there. He actually had good experiences there. He lived with a German family and they named one of their children after him. When he returned, he brought Polish sausages with him, the taste of which is still with me. (Heike actually found some of these sausages for me later and the taste was exactly the same.)

We moved to Halberstadt when he changed jobs. In Halberstadt, he worked at another airplane factory, in transportation and logistics. He took trips to Berlin as part of this job. Germany didn't really have assembly lines, but there was an effort to do something similar. Forklifts were totally unknown in Germany and my dad introduced them to factories there. I do remember him telling us that this was a useless war because the Americans produced so many more airplanes than Germany did. Later on, I read in my mother's memoirs that he had been briefed about the production capabilities of Germany during the war as compared to America and England and he saw that there was no hope. That was a dangerous thing to say out loud because by that point, just like in East Germany later on, you were spied upon by everyone. I think it was an act of courage to confide his whole attitude about the war to me.

Herbert Krippendorff with his newborn children

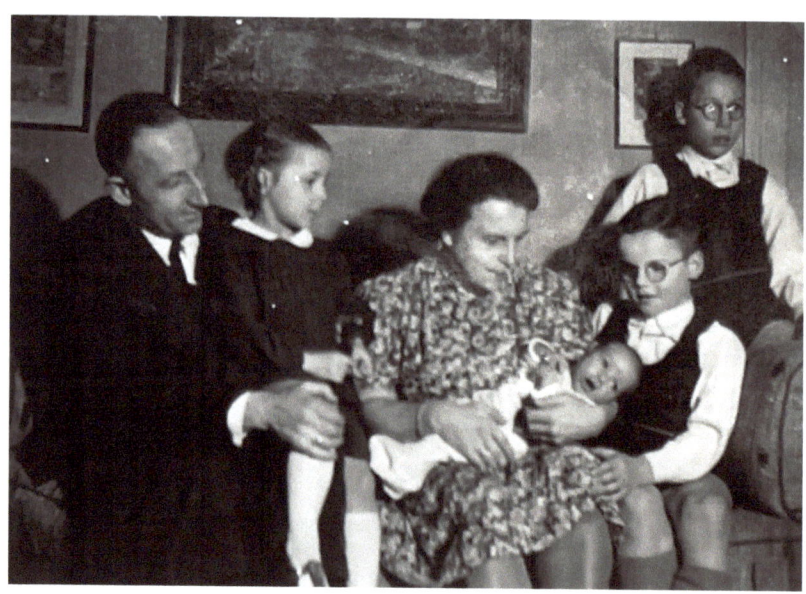

The four Krippendorff children with their grandparents

Section 1: Family History and Early Childhood

Family vacations

Lotte Krippendorff with her three eldest children, Klaus, Ekkehart, and Ute

A family celebration. In the background hangs the painting of Dresden that survived the war and that Klaus brought with him to the United States

Klaus in the countryside, possibly at Sonneck Haus

Section 2

From Halberstadt to Ratingen

Halberstadt

Halberstadt was really the city where I grew up. It's where I was from even though I wasn't born there. We moved there when I was eight years old and it's where I developed my roots. In my experience, when a child is about ten, he begins to find his own way and wean himself off the family unit. Before that he always runs behind his mother. In Halberstadt, I had a bicycle and friends; I explored the city and had adventures. Of course, there was my school, the Gymnasium Martineum, which I loved and where we learned about the history of Halberstadt and the old stories of everything around us. For example, in front of the Lutheran Dome there is a very strange, flat stone. It's huge, maybe the diameter of my apartment. How did it get there? Where is it from? What's its significance? There hangs a rusty medieval sword on the side of the Catholic church, and a lamp on the tower of the dome. There are stories about everything in Halberstadt and I know most of them. I think I know more stories about Halberstadt than about Philadelphia, and I've lived in Philadelphia now for over fifty years. Halberstadt was my city.

It was founded as a bishop's seat in the early 800s. There was a wall surrounding its residence, two churches, a Catholic church, a Protestant dome (most certainly built later), and buildings for personnel, probably monks. It was just a defensive stone wall typical of medieval times. A town grew around this original wall over the centuries, so citizens built a second, bigger wall. By the time we lived in Halberstadt, the city had grown much beyond this wall. When we moved to Halberstadt most people lived outside the second wall, as my family did. The area inside the wall was the old town. Halberstadt had about 56,000 inhabitants when I was a boy.

In addition to the Catholic and several Protestant churches, the city had also a French church. I learned much later that it was built by Huguenots who had settled in Halberstadt when they were persecuted in France. Halberstadt must have been a city open to different religions and that was unusual. This brings me to the next religious group in Halberstadt, the Jews. Jews began to arrive in Halberstadt in the 14th and 15th centuries. After one pogrom in Halle, a much larger city about seventy-five miles away, the then-bishop in Halberstadt offered the Halle Jews a place to stay. Many of them came. They probably had to pay taxes to the bishop for being protected, but it was the start of a new life, and at one point it became the largest Jewish community in Germany. Halberstadt had a synagogue and a center for Jewish studies nearby. There was a whole area of Halberstadt's old town, full of narrow streets, that was pretty much exclusively a Jewish neighborhood. I learned later that a tiny street I knew of as "Crooked Alley" was originally called the "Jewish Alley." Its name had been changed by the Nazis, who were trying to erase all references to the Jewish inhabitants and their role in Halberstadt.

I learned that the Jewish inhabitants in Halberstadt had been relatively well off and sought to escape the feared persecution. Before our time there was a project by a Catholic organization that helped get the children of Jewish families to a summer camp on the North Sea while the parents looked for new homes outside of Germany, in the Netherlands, France, or England. The program was called KLAUS, the acronym for *Kinder Lieber Auser Sicht* (in English, "children better out of sight"). It speaks to the religious tolerance in Halberstadt that a Catholic organization arranged something like this. Many of Halberstadt's Jews left thanks to this kind of program and were able to survive the Holocaust.

I didn't know anything about Jews or Judaism when I was a boy. During the Nazi time in Germany, any trace of them was removed. In fairness, I didn't know anything about Luther either even though we were technically Lutherans. Religion played no role in our family, except at Christmas when my mother took us children to church so my father could stay home to secretly set up the tree—which we always thought had appeared through magic. (It wasn't until many years later, when I happened to be in Malmö, Sweden, to give a lecture at the University, that I learned of an exhibition about Luther. I happened to have some time on my hands, and I was curious. For the first time, I really started getting interested in Luther and began to admire him for his opposition to the patriarchy of the Catholic Church, against tithes and other fees the church imposed on its members to be well received in heaven. Luther preached that everyone had to find their own way to God. I was very impressed with his revolutionary concept during his time. It started the reformation of religious life in much of Europe, but unfortunately, also war.)

My first memory of seeing a Jew was when I was walking home from school one day and I saw a couple dressed all in black; the man wore a funny hat, and both wore a yellow star. I had no idea what that was about, so I asked my mother. She said, "Those are Jews." There was no hostility in her expression, and no further explanation either. And they were the only Jewish people I had ever seen in Halberstadt. That must have been in 1942 or shortly before, because I later learned that this was the year the remainder of the Jewish population in Halberstadt was deported. I read that they were rounded up in the middle of the night, brought to an administrative office near the church, made to hand over their apartment keys, then shipped away and never seen again. Most of the Jewish population of Halberstadt was already gone by then, but there were still several hundred Jews left. The synagogue had long been "declared unsafe" and demolished. I think the reason for rounding up the remaining Jews during the night or in the very early morning when few if anybody could see it was to avoid publicity and arousal of disapproval. I like to think that Halberstadt, historically open to religions of all kinds, would have opposed this activity, but the truth is that during the Nazi regime, opposition was virtually unheard of.

Later, I asked my parents about the deportations of the Jewish population and the Holocaust: what did they know? Between 1920 and 1924, my father was in a fraternity in Dresden, where he experienced the Austrian branch of this fraternity pressuring them not to accept Jewish members. My father's fraternity resisted and severed contacts with the Austrian fraternities. But this was well before Hitler came to power. They blamed the Austrians for such discrimination. Neither of my parents were politically engaged nor I would say savvy. Early on, my mother was active in a musical association in Dresden, and she played an instrument. She had a Jewish boyfriend in that association who moved to Switzerland. She left the group because it began to ask everyone about their religious affiliation and it didn't want to have Jewish members. She was naive, as many of her friends were, about the growing antisemitism at that time, but told me a few snippets. One related to our move from Rostock to Halberstadt. When she was shown the apartment into which we eventually moved, she met the previous tenants sitting on boxes and suitcases. They were Jewish and moving to Holland. She didn't tell me how she knew that they were Jewish. At that time many better-off German Jews were moving to the Netherlands, France, and England to escape the mounting uncertainty of their future, though the Netherlands and France turned out to be not particularly safe either. Another snippet: when I asked her what she knew about the deportation of Halberstadt Jews, she told me of an acquaintance who worked for an elderly lady living below us. She came to work very early in the morning and told my mother that she had witnessed Jews being rounded up. Nobody knew what happened to them. There was no newspaper account. Opposition was not tolerated, but people could see and judge for themselves.

My godmother and my father were both from Dresden and met again in the U.S., where she studied and my father worked. My godmother was from an educated family and was a good friend of Friedrich Nietzsche's sister. She married an economist (who was a student of the famous sociologist Max Weber) about the same time my parents married. He was Jewish and already in 1933 they were preparing to leave Germany for Brazil. She told me later that my father discouraged them from leaving, telling them that Hitler and his supporters marching on the streets could not possibly govern the country and that Nazism would blow over. Obviously, my father was completely wrong. His judgment was that of an intellectual, or of bourgeois *naïveté,* unable to envision something like what happened later.

Our apartment was in a row of five-story apartment buildings on the *Moltkrdtraße 53*. Each row house had a garden in the back that was largely attended by the owner. We lived on the fourth floor in a roomy three-bedroom apartment. Every tenant had a basement room where we kept items not currently in use, but most importantly, it had shelves where my mother stored glass containers of preserved fruits and vegetables she made during the summer. Our apartment was near a park that housed a girls' gymnasium (a school, not a gym), the Lyzeum. The street was lined with trees and several of my friends lived on this street or nearby. I had good friends. We were a little gang of three or four and we climbed trees, played soccer at a garage that no longer had cars, and explored the holes in fences that led to other people's gardens—gardens from which we were often chased out. We created a lot of things. At one time we explored whether we could communicate across the street by means of a long wire stretched from our apartment window to that of my friend's, tied to cans on both ends. As long as the wire was tight, we felt we could talk to each other.

In Germany, you go through elementary school until you are ten years old. Then, you go either to a high school, called a gymnasium, or you stay in regular school until you are fourteen, at which point you are educated for a specific profession, like a plumber or electrician. When I turned ten years old I started at a gymnasium, the Martineum. This was a school emphasizing the natural sciences, Greek, Latin, philosophy, and sports. Both the education and I excelled at the Martineum.

When I wasn't playing with friends I had some fun hobbies that kept me busy. I became interested in swimming. I actually became a lifeguard and was certified to do that (this is in connection with the *Jungvolk*, which I'll get to soon). I collected stamps and built mechanical structures like cranes or cars with metal strips and screws from a versatile kit called Trix (though my Trix creations date back to Rostock rather than Halberstadt). I built a cable car once. This is where my creativity was; I was always creative. I built things not by prescription or recipe, which sometimes got me into difficulties. I built things I invented myself that interested me. I built a crane that went up and down out of the window and managed to get it to go all the way down from the fourth floor to the sidewalk. When I was playing with this crane, I saw a man sitting in a wheelchair and he had a gun in his hand. It didn't matter to me that he had a gun, but it turned out that he committed suicide. The police wanted to know if anyone had seen him handling a gun. Since I had, my mother and I went to the police station to tell them what I knew, which wasn't much. I was maybe eight or nine.

We assembled paper airplanes from cut-out sheets, which I hung from the ceiling. I eventually learned to make these on my own, but my father is the one who got me into it. I dreamed of being a pilot during the war. (My mother told me that was impossible due to my wearing glasses. I am still enthusiastic about the idea of flying. If I could, I would like to go parachuting, but I'm too old for that now.)

Another activity was music. My father's sister was a violin teacher, and she always criticized our family for being unmusical. I guess this was the motivation for us to learn an instrument. I started on a piano. I enjoyed it to a point. My teacher hit my head with a pencil each time I made a mistake. Today, this teaching method—basically avoiding mistakes without rewarding success—makes no sense. Then, I simply hated going to that teacher. My parents found another teacher with a totally different philosophy. I opted for the flute as the teacher was kind of handicapped and could not sit next to a piano student. We were scheduled for a lesson but there were other students around, and without deviating much from individual attention, she managed to have everyone collaborate. It was really more of a social phenomenon. This was far more fun to me. My brother Ekkehart started to learn the violin with that same teacher. He continued to play the violin later, but complained that this teacher ruined his playing the violin because she was more focused on encouraging collaboration and enjoying it rather than achieving individual excellence.

Wartime Activities and Jungvolk

During the war there were several public activities we were expected to engage in. Everybody had to do something to help someone else. This was actually a good idea as it created a sense of responsibility for the community.

My mother was approached by the *Frauenschaft,* an organization of women, to collect breast milk from mothers who had extra and deliver it to mothers who didn't have enough. She also once volunteered to work at a factory so some workers could have a vacation.

There was the idea at the time in Germany that mothers were to be celebrated, protected, and supported. One part of this was to learn what we'd call home economics. Young girls who wanted to teach home economics were required to spend six months in a family with children. By having four young children, my mother qualified to "teach" a young student what it took to raise children and run a household. The girls did all the things my mother did and learned enough to receive a sort of certificate that showed she could do this work. We had two different students stay with us. The first one was Christel, who was from a nearby village, Schwanebeck, and unknowingly established a connection for us to her family that proved to be a lifesaver after the bombing of Halberstadt.

I had jobs too. One was to bring up a bucket of coal from the basement a couple times a week to our elderly neighbor. Another was to meet refugees from the east of Germany, from East Prussia, Silesia, and the Baltic countries (who were fleeing the Russian advances), at the train station and direct them to wherever they were finding temporary shelter in Halberstadt. (My parents became good friends with a couple from Estonia in this way.) We would also go from house to house to ask if anyone had spare clothes to give to the refugees. Annually there was a drive to collect contributions to what was called *Winterhilfswerk des Deutschen Volkes* (Winter Relief of the German People). A contributor received a small gift like a small glass amulet with the face of a famous philosopher, poet, or political figure engraved on it, or a memorial brown clay coin made by the famous Meissen porcelain manufacture. I still have a couple of those. As the threat of bombing grew, I was assigned the job of messenger. As messenger I wore a blue armband with an "M" on it. The idea was, if there was a fire, I would be the one who went and reported it. I would have to report any casualties and ask for help. However, when Halberstadt was bombed, everything collapsed with it, so it was a job I never did.

Next to my family and activities at home, my friends, the school, other assignments, and music, there was my experience in the Jungvolk. Starting in 1936, every child at the age of ten was drafted in the state-organized youth organizations. Boys entered the *Deutsche Jungvolk* (DJ), and girls became members of the *Jungmädelbund*. The *Jungvolk* was to Hitler Youth like Cub Scouts were to Boy Scouts—except the German youth organization was obligatory, designed to encourage discipline and loyalty to the state, which traditional schools did not guarantee. After the age of fourteen, boys became members of the Hitler Youth (HJ) and girls became members of the *Bund Deutscher Mädel* (BDM). All of these levels of organization were hierarchically organized, like in the military. In the *Jungvolk* you started as a *Pimpf*. About ten boys formed a *Jungenschaft*, about four *Jungenschaften* formed a *Jungzug*, four *Jungzug* formed a *Fähnlein*. Halberstadt had ten *Fähnlein*; half of then formed a *Stamm*. Each unit had a single leader. Mine was *Fähnlein 9* and we met every Wednesday and Saturday afternoon. We played sports. We marched a lot to drums and trumpets. I enjoyed the rhythm of the drums when we marched, but it was always the same pattern. I thought at some point, *I can do a different rhythm, one that we could march to as well*. I asked to play the drum but after using a different beat, I was never allowed to drum again. The other thing we did was sing in groups, at times competing with other units of the *Jungvolk*. Canons were good among the four *Jungenschaften* of a *Jungzug*. We sang songs we learned without caring much about their content. I recognize only now how much they were intended to ideologically frame us. They were songs about fighting our enemies, about strength derived from following leaders. We were unaware of how this content could have structured our thinking. The only activity I abhorred was when we were asked to physically fight each other, one *Fähnlein* against another. I did it when I had to, but I keep a bad memory of it. The fighting, the hierarchical organization, and the disciplined marching in groups were all designed to prepare us for an autocratic state and military service.

I want to mention an experience of an opposite kind. It started with an earlier leader of our *Jungzug* joining us on his vacation while we were marching to and then playing in a hilly area very close by, the *Spiegelsberge*. I had often gone there, including with my parents.

On this particular day, that former leader took us to a place of white sand surrounded by walls of rocks. He fed our curiosity by telling us he knew of the entrance to a cave, which, the story said, went from where we stood all the way to the dome in Halberstadt. These caves had been used in medieval times to get in and out of Halberstadt when it was besieged by a hostile army. (I'm not sure that was true.)

We agreed that on our next meeting we'd all come with a shovel. That day we showed up and all started digging. It went on like that for a while but then we heard a loud thump when one of the shovels hit something different. It was a wood plank. We uncovered more dirt and sand and saw it was several planks that constituted the entrance to a cave.

We pulled back the wood and all we could see was a steep path going down into the ground. It was dark and narrow and clearly dangerous. I remember the first time I stood there looking down and the thought that went through my head was, *Do we have to go down there?* Of course, we went. In fact, we went many, many times. We explored the caves and it was incredibly exciting and fun. It was one of the most important experiences of my youth.

Some of the underground caves were big rooms with walkways and openings that we had to climb through. Other parts we had to half crawl, half drag ourselves through on our stomachs because the ceiling was so low. We never knew what was on the other side of a tunnel. Often we didn't have a choice but to go forward because it simply wasn't possible to turn back. For flashlights we used a candle in a tin can. With that, we went through these caves again and again. It was fascinating. It felt like we owned them, we knew them so well.

Toward the end of the war, maybe in '44, there was an effort to build a bunker in the caves to protect the population from bombings. I remember we were down there once and heard officials talking at a distance. We froze. The voices were getting louder as they came our way. They didn't know we were there. We waited until they were close and then we ran right by them. We knew we had to get out because they would have caught us. That event ended the attraction of the caves for us.

This was the city and setting of my youth. The war did not affect us negatively. My parents were skiers and wanted, among other things, to go skiing, so they put us in a kids' camp. I remember it clearly, though I was still young. Some of the other children there were from Berlin and we heard stories of bombings. A few of them wet their beds out of fright of not seeing their parents again. Even with food rationing, the hardships of war were not something I remember as a problem in our lives until Germany began to lose the war. My mother would sometimes ride her bike to Schwanebeck and get apples and cherries from Christel's family. My father was never drafted so our family wasn't separated and damaged in that way. His work at the factory kept him safe from that, even though he had to officially join the Nazi party. They told him plainly that if he didn't join the Nazi party, he would be sent to the front. He didn't want to but that was the condition of staying at the factory.

The Bombing

Airplanes flew over Germany all the time. Sometimes only a single one came to explore, other times it was a squadron of three hundred. We all had basements that were reinforced, meaning they put a wooden beam in the middle like in coal mines and then a big beam on top. If the house collapsed, you would be safe. In theory. Another thing was that every house—it was all rowhomes of small apartment buildings—had to have access to the next house so if you were completely trapped, there was a way to get to the next house and escape. These were some of the precautions that existed for the safety of the population.

Another precaution was sirens. Sirens warned when airplanes were coming. There were two levels of sirens: one was a warning and the other meant there was real danger. All the time at night, with our blankets over our shoulders, we had to go to the basement four levels down and stay there until the airplanes passed. At times like that all the neighbors—everybody—was down there. Our basement was below street level on one side, but the other side, where the garden was located, was almost at street level, and you could see a little of what was going on outside.

During air raids we could learn the position of the airplanes on the radio. Maps had quadrants and Halberstadt was J6. The radio would say, "The planes are moving from J5 to J6," or such, so we knew just what was in the air and where. When Dresden was bombed in February of 1945, they didn't mention the quadrants, they just said more specifically, "Dresden is under attack." My parents were shocked when it happened. Dresden was a target because everyone apparently converged in Dresden. It was bombed several times. Lots of German refugees, fleeing the Russians, came from the east by train. Dresden was actually overpopulated and many of them burned to death. (My father decided to go to Dresden after the bombing to look for his relatives, though he couldn't get into the city.)

The bombings were very strategic. First came explosives that opened up everything and then came firebombs. Firebombs were like sticks with wicks in the middle. You could handle them before the wicks exploded the bomb. My favorite aunt, Dorle, was married to a merchant whose house in Dresden we had visited many times. During the bombing, Aunt Dorle ran up to her attic and grabbed some of the firebombs that had fallen in there and quickly threw them out of the window. Dorle was very good at this and it seemed like she had saved the house. However, many of the neighboring houses started to burn. These fires soon became so forceful that her own curtains caught on fire. She ran from room to room, ripping down the curtains in order to prevent the fire from spreading. It didn't help. In the end, she had to flee.

In addition to the firebombs and explosive bombs, there were napalm bombs. Napalm is a fluid, and when used in a bomb it spreads like water and creates a very hot fire. When that happened in Dresden you couldn't go on the street. Each house had a little garden, like here in Philadelphia, enclosed with steel fences. People would hold on to the steel fence and walk on the edge of the fence from garden to garden so they didn't step in the napalm. Dresden had a big zoo, which was also bombed. The tigers escaped and had to be shot. My aunts Dorle and Hilde found refuge in the outskirts of Dresden when this all happened.

I was not afraid when I heard sirens. Air raids were overwhelming to me, not terrifying. Another interesting thing in retrospect is when my father was in Poland, he brought home with him Polish steel helmets, which were a very different shape than the German ones. We had them in the basement with us. I should have worn mine for protection, but I never did.

One family in our building had evacuated to Halberstadt because the American army was approaching in the west. There was a mother, a daughter, and the daughter's baby. They were solid Catholics and had been bombed out of their previous home. During one of the bombings, they came to our basement area and the baby couldn't breathe. You have never experienced anything like this unless you live through it. Dust is not just dust. It is thick particles of sand, dirt—everything. You can hardly breathe. The mother saw that the baby was not breathing any more from all the dust. My father was forty-five years old and he knew what to do. He took charge. He dunked the baby's head in a water bucket, then gave it back to her, and the baby was fine. I remember the mother started saying prayers in the highest voice when the baby began to breathe again.

We were down there almost every night, always with our blankets. There was some sort of bunk bed to sleep in, but we didn't sleep because the sirens and bombs were nerve wracking. My mother decided at some point that she needed to have a bit of time away from this. She took my three siblings to Schwanebeck to stay with Christel's mother. My father and I stayed behind in Halberstadt.

One morning, I went to a friend's house a couple blocks away. He collected stamps like I did, and we would look at our stamp collections and make trades. On this particular day, April 8, 1945, it was a Sunday morning.

At about eleven o'clock we heard the warning alarm, so I went home immediately. As soon as I got home the second alarm began, and not long after that we could hear the airplanes. We went down to the basement as usual. My father looked out the garden side of the basement to try and see the planes. He saw the markers coming down for where the bombers were going to lay their bombs. When he came back in he said, "This is it. This is the one." One bomb fell about twelve yards from where my father was, and I waited.

When the bombs and explosions stopped, I can't say that I was shocked. I knew we were alive. We wanted to get out of the basement so we went upstairs, but we had to climb out of a window to get to the street. There was no front door anymore. The bomb took half of our apartment building down.

Now, this street was *my* street. I knew every tree from climbing them with my friends, every part of the sidewalk, every house. It was no longer recognizable. Most of the houses were crumpled heaps. The street was full of bricks. Everything was piles of bricks and stones. It is very difficult to walk over piles of bricks; you can't get your footing and there is no stability. I walked from our crumbled house toward an area that was a park. My father went upstairs to the fourth floor, into the au

The painting of Dresden Klaus kept in his home his whole life

pair girl's room where we had our shoes in the cupboard. He took sheets from the bed, put all the shoes in there, and took it down to the basement. The only other item he took from our house was the painting of Dresden that hangs in my dining room today. These were the things that were saved.

Then, our house started to burn so he found another house and tried to deposit things there. For some reason he decided he needed to go into the old part of Halberstadt. He instructed me to go to the girls' gymnasium at the park and wait for him there. I said OK, but I didn't do that. First, I went toward the end of our block where one of my best friends lived. I wanted to go in there and see how it was. His house was also bombed. The stairs were wooden stairs, and they had collapsed so I had to walk over the edges of the stairs. I saw a few other people there. Suddenly the noise of another bombing came. There was no more siren to alert us. Everything was under attack or already destroyed.

What happened next was an interesting experience. When people are so afraid they don't really know what to do, they bundle together. I was simply with a group of people huddled together. One woman had dug herself out of the rubble and had almost nothing on; she was naked from the waist down. There were five or six people and we huddled there, simply clumped in a group. At some point, I looked up, and I saw that half of the house was hanging over us. It could have easily fallen down without any sort of shaking. We quickly went away from there. Luckily the bombing didn't seem to target this part of the city anymore and the planes grew more distant. I walked over to the park where I found people from our house and others. This is where I was supposed to meet my father.

This park was designated as a kind of safe space, because a park is not a structure that you can destroy in the way you can destroy a building. But this was one experience I never forgotten. I had to pee. This park had bushes about eight feet high, but they had been flattened to the ground from the force of the bombs. That's where I went to pee. I saw a bird there. It had been pushed into the ground and couldn't fly, but it was alive.

I was prepared to wait for my father at this park, but the people I was with said I couldn't stay there. They said that when the fire came it would suck me into it. The fire would advance faster than I could run. That convinced me. I joined them and we walked away from there. I do distinctly remember a man standing on a fallen tree trunk and his jaw was gone. He didn't know what to do. He was standing there, and I saw it. We walked for a bit and reached the areas with the caves where

I so often played. I looked back toward Halberstadt, and I could see the whole city on fire with flames the size of houses and a huge black smoke column rising above it. It was a sight I'll never forget.

None of us knew what to do so we kept walking until we reached a village. There was a farmer there and he opened up his barn to us. He cooked us a meal so we had something to eat in the evening, and then we slept directly on the hay. When I woke up the next day, I decided I needed to find my family so I left this group and headed to Schwanebeck alone.

Meanwhile, my parents were frantically looking for me. Schwanebeck was only eleven kilometers from Halberstadt. When he couldn't find me and the city burned, he went to Schwanebeck and told my mother that I was lost. Before that, my mother had already rode her bicycle from Schwanebeck to Halberstadt to look for us but couldn't go to the house because of the fires. When she turned around to return to Schwanebeck, a woman asked her to take two small children with her while the woman stayed behind in Halberstadt. My mother walked her bicycle the whole way home with these two children on it, who cried almost the entire time. Those poor children with a complete stranger, not knowing where they were going, and their mother gone... it was terrible. They were picked up later that night by someone, though. That's when my father got there and reported that I was lost. It wasn't until the day after that, that I arrived in Schwanebeck. I kind of knew the terrain and was able to make my way there without getting lost. At some point during my walk to Schwanebeck, there were airplanes above and I remember hiding under a farmer's big wooden cart. I was very afraid. I was definitely shocked from the experience, maybe in shock, but I don't think it lasted that long.

Schwanebeck

When I got to Schwanebeck on Monday, I found my parents and siblings pretty quickly. They were with the family of Christel, our old au pair girl, and we were able to stay in the tiny, tiny house of Christel's grandmother. There was an area upstairs under the roof with one little room. All of us slept in there. It was almost impossible, but we had to do it. We had no choice. And luckily, they allowed us to do it. From the front yard of that house, we watched a munitions train get bombarded and the explosions were enormous. There was a ditch next to the side of the road and I crawled in there because I needed to feel some protection. My mother said in her memoirs that I was in shock and couldn't stand the noise of the bombs.

Christel's grandmother was devastated. She was a Nazi, a real Nazi. She had pictures of Hitler everywhere in the house. When the German soldiers came through on the run from the Americans, she took all the pictures of Hitler down and hid them. The German soldiers said not to worry, and they were right. The Americans came after the Germans, but nothing happened. When the Americans approached Schwanebeck, of course we were afraid, and we hid in the basement. There were one or two shots fired, blind shots in the direction of the village. When there was no response, the Americans came through. One truck after another of American soldiers rolled in. They were very nice and gave us leftover rations. One interesting thing was that I had never seen Black people until then, and suddenly I was seeing lots of Black people. I asked my parents, "Why do the Black people all drive the cars?" My parents said it was because they were better drivers. Prejudice didn't work with my parents.

This was April 11. The Americans just moved on through and it was the American occupation. They took over one hotel in the little town, a very small hotel, and they needed a cleaning woman. They met with the mayor, who was actually a communist, and the brother of our Nazi hosts. The brothers hated each other, of course, and didn't talk. The mayor knew that my mother had a home economics teaching certificate and designated her to be a cleaning woman in this hotel. Of course, she could speak English well and that helped her tremendously.

With Halberstadt bombed and the war basically over, my father had nothing to do anymore. And we needed money. He had a great idea: he could repair agriculture equipment that was neglected or destroyed during the war. He knew there was a train close to Schwanebeck that had machines for military production that was sitting there not doing anything. He was able to convince the American commander that he should get some of these machines in order to open a repair shop. He then hired some farmers with cows and carts, and they got a few machines out of there. He found an empty storage place and they opened it up for to him start this mechanical workshop. There were maybe two or three machines. One was a lathe. Soon his business was doing work for the local farmers, who quickly appreciated him because he was helping them fix their farming equipment.

People sometimes ask how I lived through the war and the bombing without being traumatized. In truth, it didn't really harm me that much. I think it was in large part because my family was together. We were always a family. My parents were pro-American in every respect. They owned books in English, though they hid them on the shelves behind other German books during the war. My parents spoke English to each other before the war and one of their fears was that, if my bother or I were asked, we would not be able to lie and we'd say that they spoke English. They didn't believe the Nazi propaganda. My father joined the Nazi party to avoid being sent to the front. They knew they had to play by rules in order to survive, and we did survive.

The Russians

The area where we lived was given to the Russians when Germany was split up after the war. Soon the Americans left, the Russians came, and there was a great difference in the occupation of Germany. One morning, we saw a red flag on top of the church. The Russians entered Schwanebeck, in comparison to the Americans, much differently. They had little wooden carts that sat two people, drawn by one horse—an endless row of these carts. That's how they came through as opposed to the Americans, with their tanks and trucks.

My father's work continued. One challenge was finding materials to make repairs at his shop, for example, sheet metal. He went, among other places, to Halberstadt to try to locate the materials he needed. On one trip there, he ran into a former employee of his airplane factory, from before the war. This former employee had been a driver in the factory, bringing tools and materials from one place to another in little electric cars. But he was a very unreliable worker; in fact, he was often drunk. He would flirt with women from the East and harass them. At some point, my father had to talk to him and tell him he couldn't do that. Now here they were, after the war, and my father and this man talked and told each other what they were doing. My father learned that his former boss was in prison in Halberstadt. My father said he was sorry to hear that, but it was an important piece of information because he knew he could have been in prison also and was lucky that he wasn't. They then said goodbye and my father came home.

Two days later, a Russian truck came to Schwanebeck, picked up my father, and took him to the prison in Halberstadt. Who opened the door of the prison? This former employee from the airplane factory.

**MECHANISCHE WERKSTATT SCHWANEBECK
KRIPPENDORFF**

ERSATZTEILEFERTIGUNG FÜR LANDWIRTSCHAFTLICHE MASCHINEN

Postscheck-Konto: Magdeburg Nr. 23917
Bank-Konto: Stadt-Sparbank Schwanebeck
Fernsprech-Anschluß: Schwanebeck Nr. 14

Schwanebeck, den
Oschersleber Straße 32

Letterhead from Klaus's father's business after the war

Section 2: From Halberstadt to Ratingen

My mother was left alone in charge and had a lot to manage. She had four children to take care of, the youngest being Rainer, who was two years old. That's very demanding even when there is no war. I was thirteen years old. She also had the mechanical workshop to oversee. She didn't have any knowledge of mechanics, but she was a bookkeeper and she had good common sense. My father had already hired several people from the factories. They could manage the machines and continued to work there. Like that, she was able to keep the workshop alive.

She would regularly ride her bicycle to Halberstadt to take food and a change of clothes to the prison for my father. She never saw him, but she was assured that he would get what she left for him, and she got the message later on that he did in fact get her packages. But then my father was transported to a prison in Magdeburg, which was about fifty kilometers away. She rode her bicycle there a few times, with food and clothes. The last time she went, they said they couldn't accept anything. Nonetheless, she convinced them to give it to him. They accepted it but he never saw it. It's amazing the things she did for him and us.

My mother used to say that my father took things differently than most. He was well educated, even though an engineer and a technical person, but he went to a gymnasium and had a classical education. He knew all of Shakespeare and other classical things like that. He organized among the prisoners not the reading of Shakespeare, but reciting it. Whatever anyone could contribute they did. He basically made an educational situation out of being locked up. He was an amazing prisoner.

The Baracke

With my father in prison in Magdeburg, there were only five of us left in this tiny, tiny attic, but it was still not a long-term living solution. One day, along came the mayor, the communist, who of course was now on top of everything going on in this little town. He told us that we had to find a better place to live. Not far away, there was a former storage area made out of prefabricated buildings. We called it the *baracke*. There were four spaces there for people to live. My mother and I went to see it, and I remember there were lice all over the floors. Construction materials were stored there, but he said we could have one of the spaces. There would have to be a door put in and walls

Our 'Baracke' in Schwanebeck

The Krippendorff residence 1945 – 1949. It started with being shown one of four one-floor empty spaces, containing building materials. I (Klaus at the age of 13) designed the interior space while our father was in a Russian prison. The following was reconstructed from memory on 2022.05.11 aided by old photos and talking with my brother Rainer who visited the place before its replacement.

We were offered the 3rd of four empty spaces, 6^2 meter = 9.6^2 feet in size, and 10 panels to divide the space: | | | | | | | | | | ↕1 m each, and 4 doors.
The 2nd unit was already partitioned into four equally sized rooms, intended for all units.
(I opted to retrieve an 11th panel from one exterior panel, replaced by a door.)

The main objective was to get a larger living room with the kitchen and access to the outhouse without having to go around the building. My parents and the two smaller children, initial age 2 and 7, slept in the larger bedroom, Ekkehart and I, initially 11 and 13, slept in the smaller.

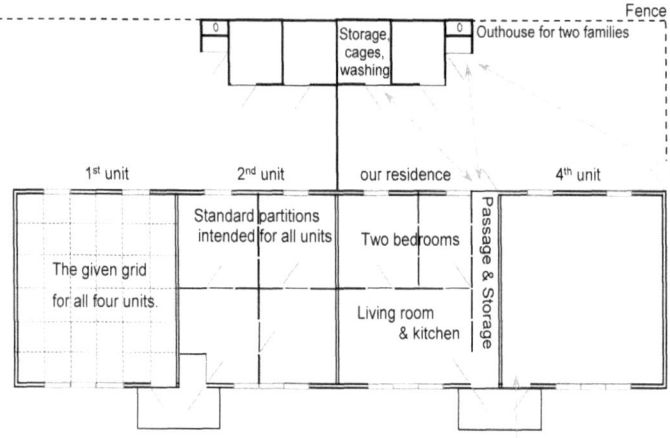

There was no running water in most of the village of Schwanebeck. Shoulder carried water carriers

We got water in canisters from a nearby hand pumped well, meant to serve the adjacent cemetery.

The outhouse was in the back of the house, shared with the neighboring family in the 4th unit.

The outside storage room contained cages for rabbits, bins for chickens that laid eggs, and a wood-fired kettle for washing the laundry, hanged to dry on a line between the two structures.

We dug an earth-covered ≈ 6 feet deep trench in front of the house, with an exhaust and a door leading to a ladder. It preserved perishable food items like potatoes and apples – our "refrigerator."

This was my first exposure to albeit primitive "industrialized architecture" !

Klaus documented the baracke though it is not likely the size was actually six square meters

built. Some guy gave us four doors and some partitions and told us to design what we needed. My mother assigned that task to me.

Working on this *baracke* was my first architectural accomplishment. I have to say, in retrospect, that I'm surprised my mother trusted a thirteen-year-old boy to design the space. I still don't understand it; I wouldn't do that. The space was six square meters (9.6 square feet), and we had ten panels of one meter in height to divide the space, and four doors.[1] The second unit was already partitioned into four equally sized rooms, as it was intended for all the units. There was also a little cubicle at the entrance so that the front door would not open directly onto the street. I thought that this was not going to be a helpful setup. The toilets were outside toilets, and they were in the back of the *baracke*. In their design you had to exit from the front of the *baracke* and walk all the way around the building to get to the outhouse. I thought, *why don't we make a corridor from the front of our space to the back, with an exit in the back?* My main objective was to get a larger living room with the kitchen and access to the outhouse without having to go outside around the building. We made only three rooms instead of four: one big one for the family, and two rooms to sleep. I made the drawing, and I gave it to this guy. He could only give us a certain number of these partitions and no more, but I was within his limit and it was our choice if we wanted to use the materials differently than the sample unit. It was a fabulous design. My mother and the two smaller children slept in the larger room. Ekkehart and I slept in the smaller room. We lived there for quite some time.

There was no running water in most of the village of Schwanebeck. Shoulder-carried water carriers were used to get water from a nearby hand-pumped well that was meant to serve the adjacent cemetery. The outside storage area contained cages for rabbits, bins for chickens that laid eggs, and a wood-fired kettle for washing the laundry, which was hung to dry on a line between the two structures. We dug an earth-covered, six-foot-deep trench in front of the house, with an exhaust and a door leading to a ladder. Our "refrigerator" preserved perishable food items like potatoes and apples. Albeit primitive, this was my first exposure to "industrialized architecture"!

We didn't have much food. There were no grocery stores. What we call a supply chain was nonexistent. We had good relationships with some of the farmers because my father worked with them to repair their equipment. We got jobs working for these farmers, picking potatoes. They paid us in vegetables. The farmers also allowed us to go to their fields after harvest and pick any potatoes still in the ground. That's one thing that we did very systematically. Another thing is

---

[1] It is likely that the baracke was larger than that. Although Klaus left a sketch of the baracke with this measurement, six square meters is simply not possible, even for the times.

we would trade whatever we could find, like canned fish that was sometimes given out at a train depot. We got some fish and traded it for other things. Because Germany was cut off from the international trade, there was no sugar. However, there were sugar turnips that were grown in the area, and there was a big sugar factory that made sugar out of that. Crates of these turnips often fell off the back of trucks and we collected them. My mother managed to make syrup that way. We were all very, very connected with nature for our survival.

Among the chickens we also had a rooster. He was very aggressive. When we went to the outhouse the rooster would attack us; Ekkehart remembers this, too. I would take a stick with me to defend myself. One time, I remember distinctly that I hit that rooster very hard and almost killed it. I still can see that rooster lying on the ground struggling, horizontal, and I felt really bad. This is one lesson that I kept always: when you have the might, like I did with the stick, it's a mistake to use all the power that you have. I could have hit that rooster more defensively; I didn't have to hit it that hard. In the end, we had to slaughter the rooster and eat it.

How did we feed the chickens? We were able to get leftover grain from harvest so we gave that to the chickens, but my mother invented something very clever to give the chickens more food. She collected horse manure from the street, put it in a can with holes on the underside, and hung it up where the chickens were. The horse manure attracted flies, which laid eggs that became worms, and they would eventually fall down through the holes in the bottom of the can which the chickens could eat.

While we were adjusting to life in the *baracke,* my father was being moved to a concentration camp. They loaded him and the other prisoners into a cargo wagon, all of them jammed in tightly. They were on the train until they reached their destination and it was time to be unloaded. When they got off the train my father saw heaps of calcium, the kind of material that you put over decaying bodies. It was an old Nazi concentration camp, refurnished for Russian use. He saw where he was and thought to himself, *Well, here it is, this is the end. This is where I will die.*

One by one, the names of the prisoners were called. My father waited, but his name was never called. Eventually, he was put back on the train to Magdeburg. My father didn't know what was happening.

Russians plan things by quotas. Let's say they had to deliver 100 prisoners to the concentration camp. Because some of them might die on the way, to be safe 120 are sent. On the way, not enough people died so there were too many prisoners for the camp. What to do now? Well, they were sent back, like my father, to Magdeburg.

But, with this Russian way of organizing, when you're off the books, you're off the books. He was delivered there but not killed. So now a new problem existed: where did he fit in? The next day he was called to see the commander of the prison, who said to him, "You are innocent. Tomorrow you will be freed and can be with your wife and children. But what can you give us for letting you go?" My father told him we had been bombed out and had nothing to offer. "But," he continued, "I have a mechanical workshop. I can work to repair things for the Russians. I can do my best to help with that." The next morning, he was released and took to the train back to Schwanebeck.

We were all very lucky my father was released. He soon started thinking of ways to help the family survive. One thing he did was invent a sort of crank to make oil out of poppy seeds. Poppy seeds, for whatever reason, were common in the area and there were many big fields of it around us. Someone in West Germany, a farmer, heard about my father's crank and wanted one. He offered us a piglet in return. It was decided that my mother was the one who would make the exchange, and she took me with her. We went to this farmer, stayed overnight, demonstrated this machine, and he gave us a piglet. We took the train back with the pig in a knapsack. Shortly before we came to the river on the West German border, my mother looked into the knapsack and the pig had died. We think the farmer who gave us the piglet gave it sleeping pills so it wouldn't make noises and get us in trouble with the guards. My mother had to throw it out the window. I remember this piglet plunged out the window onto the wood platform, and then tumbled over into the fields beyond. We went home without the pig. This is the type of thing we did to cope.

Dresden

At some point my mother's sister Dorle came to visit us in the *baracke*, before my father had returned. They were very, very close sisters. They were almost twins. She saw the burden on my mother and offered to take one of the children back to Dresden with her. They chose me. Dorle didn't have a good place for me to sleep, but my other aunt, my father's sister Hilde, had a son that was maybe five years older and had been drafted at the last minute into the German army and was now in a Russian prison, so she had an extra bed.

My mother's family, as I have said, was a business family. They were always laughing and making jokes. They were clumped together and did things together. They were outgoing. My father's family was very different. My grandfather was a lawyer, educated, and then an officer. His wife, my grandmother, was very regimented. When you visited her for coffee you had to be punctual. You had to be disciplined.

Hilde was older than my father. She married a man who had had a first wife. He was a medical doctor and they had three boys. (Two of them emigrated to Mexico. I visited one of them later on, but I had no connection with them really. Another one was a doctor, but was drafted into the army.) Hilde's husband was a real country doctor, with a bicycle. He took that very seriously. He had his office and he had instruments. They were all brass instruments housed behind a vitrine. He was an older guy and had been a ship doctor in the First World War. He once fell from a bicycle. Why? Because he forgot to pedal.

In any case, Hilde was just like her side of the family—very well organized, very regimented. She became a violin teacher. Music was very important to this family; everyone had to have an instrument whether you could play it or not. Her second husband was a piano player. The oldest son was a cellist. (He became a physicist.) The second son (the one in the Russian prison) played piano, too. The youngest son played cello. I stood out because I didn't play any instruments. She was really hostile to me because I didn't contribute anything music-wise. I didn't fit into that musical family. My father didn't play any instrument, nor did my mother. Thus, Hilde defined my family as unmusical. (The younger son later became a famous cellist and played in the Munich Philharmonic Orchestra as the chief cellist. The brother in the Russian prison later became a pianist and then a choreographer. He was also an artist. When he was in the Russian prison, he had scissors and he cut out paper figures, lots of them. He became increasingly good at that. I have some examples. Once he even had an exhibition of these paper cuts. In the back of the yard at my aunt's house, he had a tiny garden house where he used to hide to paint. I think it is very important to have a place where you can go and not be disturbed, so you can develop on your own.)

I was reasonably close with her younger son. My aunt would come to read stories to him before bed, and one time when I was in his room, I hid behind the bed as Hilde approached. As it turned out, she didn't read stories to him; she complained about me. She said I was a farmer's boy, meaning someone with a low education. Then she noticed me and said, "Eavesdroppers seldom hear good of themselves." This was basically my relationship with my aunt. I was there, I was tolerated, and that was it.

The Apprenticeship

School started again for me in Dresden while my father was still in prison. Luckily, I was in a gymnasium; in fact, the same that my father had gone to. There was even one teacher who my father had also had as a teacher. The main problem for me was that, as any thirteen-year-old would, I needed some encouragement. I got none.

I took the tram to school and it was quite a long ride. I made some friends and we did things together after school. Someone had found some abandoned ammunition for artillery: long sticks like macaroni, with a hole in the middle. The pieces came bundled together. We found many of them and we would ignite them by stepping on them. The fire would light up inside the hollow center, and we would throw them. We had all kinds of distractions like this that were not academic, and they were a lot more fun.

My aunt had no interest in having me do my homework. I was actually good in mathematics. I was good in biology. I could draw flowers, which was one of the things we had to do in biology class. But I hated Latin. I thought to myself, *Nobody speaks Latin. Why should I ever learn it? It's stupid.* My father knew Latin very well. Had he been available at that time, he would have told me Latin gives one access to so many things, like other languages. He would have encouraged me to stick with it. But my aunt had no interest in encouraging me. I started to tell my mom I wanted to get out of school.

At Christmas I was able to go home for the holiday and my father had just gotten back from prison. One of my older cousins had woodworking tools and I carved an angel for the top of the tree to bring home with me. (I just gave that angel to my son.) When I got home I told them I wanted to stop going to the gymnasium. They listened to me and decided to let me stop. That was a big mistake. Adults should not listen to thirteen-year-olds who are desirous of getting out of something. A child that age doesn't know what kind of decisions to make for the future. (As a side comment, much later, my youngest brother, Rainer, was not very good in high school. He too wanted to get out of it, and I told my parents not to let him. They listened to me, hired a tutor, and got him through school. He went on to study at the university. He didn't like high school, but it gave him options that mattered to him later.)

But at the time I was just happy to be back with my family. School stopped at Easter and that's when I moved back to Schwanebeck. My father knew a former engineer from before the war and I became an apprentice for that man, in Halberstadt. It was in a mechanical shop. Being an apprentice in Germany has been a tradition for hundreds of years. You become an apprentice for three years, then you become a journeyman who has the skill to establish himself. He meets a girl, becomes a master in his trade, and has his own shop. That was the path I was on. I was an apprentice in a mechanical shop for three years. The schooling aspect was minimal. It was held once a week, in the afternoon. The apprenticeship was training to become a mechanic and that was it, even though we supposedly had school too.

It was a tough job, but I was pretty good at mechanical work. There are no real stories about this time as an apprentice except for one incident. One of the journeymen in this shop stole a bicycle from a Russian. The Russian suspected that he stole the bike but didn't have any evidence. They came and investigated everything. They gathered us all together to ask us questions, and maybe out of nervousness, I laughed. That was a dangerous moment. The shopkeeper hit me hard when I laughed. My laughing was inappropriate, but it was a response of nervousness or to the absurdity of the situation. That is a very clear memory I have of that time.

Leaving East Germany

At some point, around 1948, the Russians made a law saying that all property, like machines, belonged to the state. One day the Russians came, picked up all the machines from my father's workshop, and took them away. With the machines gone he had no way to run his repair business. What was he to do now? He no longer had a way of making a living. That's when my parents decided we had to leave East Germany.

He went by himself on a trip to West Germany and met up with some of his old buddies he knew from his time in America. He spoke to them about leaving East Germany and they encouraged him. They told him he would easily be able to find a job and helped him do that. He started looking immediately and soon found a half-time job in Düsseldorf. One of his friends had a small house, like a wood shack, where we were able live temporarily. When he came back to Schwanebeck, he said we had to start making plans to leave.

My father went over with my brother first and started his new job. The plan was that the rest of us would join him, but I wanted to finish my apprenticeship. It was just a question of maybe a month or so. But Schwanebeck was a very small village where everyone knew everything about everyone else. People knew my father had been asked to join the Communist Party and that he didn't want to. They soon noticed he wasn't around, and people asked my mom where he was. She told them that he was in Dresden and that the whole family was going to move there. In order to make sure that what she said was believed, she addressed parcels to him at the post office to Dresden. Everything went to Dresden. I wasn't allowed to tell anyone we were planning on leaving, not even my best friend, whom I always took the train with from Schwanebeck to Halberstadt. I still feel bad about that.

My mother bought tickets to go to Dresden, as if she and my siblings were joining my father there. She may even have sent the children there ahead. From Dresden they made their way to Halberstadt and met with a former schoolteacher from the area near the border where we wanted to cross (nor far from Helmstedt). He knew that area very well and she hired him to get us over to West Germany. She stayed in Halberstadt with my siblings until it was time to leave, so it would look like the Krippendorffs moved to Dresden. She took care of sending our few possessions to my father. She hired a farmer with a cart to take things, like sheets and the painting of Dresden that my father had saved during the bombing, to a river near the border where my father came to get them.

I stayed in Schwanebeck to finish my apprenticeship, commuting to Halberstadt every day. Finally, it was the last day of my apprenticeship, and I would be meeting my mother in Halberstadt to leave the next day. On the last day of my apprenticeship, one of the farmers we knew was in the city hall and overheard a conversation there. Someone the farmer didn't know was asking where Herbert Krippendorff was. A clerk at city hall told the stranger that he was in Dresden. The stranger said that was not true, he was nowhere in Dresden. "Are there any other Krippendorffs in Schwanebeck? I want to see them." That evening the farmer came to tell me what he had overheard: they were looking for us. The earliest train the next morning was at 4:00 a.m., and I was on it.

I met up with my mother in Halberstadt much earlier than expected, but we left as planned. We took the train as far as we could and then met up with the teacher. We had to walk the rest of the way.

I had a bicycle with me. The air tubes inside the tires had burst a long time ago and I created a replacement for them out of discarded air pressure tubes used to connect railroad cars.

My mother, my little brother Rainer, my sister Ute, the teacher, and I walked through the German countryside at night, avoiding villages and roads so we wouldn't be seen. It was very hard to avoid villages, but we couldn't risk having someone see refugees trying to go west. We had a problem with dogs. When a dog hears a noise he starts to howl and then the other dogs hear him and join in too. We frequently triggered the howling of dogs and worried it would give us away.

By the side of the roads in the German countryside, it is common to have ditches on the other side of the trees that line the roads. The ditches are between the trees and the fields. At one point the guide heard voices and told us to quickly jump into the ditch and hide. We all jumped down in the ditch and were worried that the younger children would make noise. A couple of Russian soldiers walked by, and we waited for them to be far away before we got out of the ditch and continued our long walk.

We kept going and next came to an area with more soldiers. Of course, we were afraid, but it turned out these soldiers were British. We were finally on the other side. My mother went up to one of them and hugged him. That was unusual behavior, but she was relieved to be safe. I don't remember exactly where we crossed the border, but it was near the town of Helmstedt. We then went to the closest train station and headed to Ratingen to meet up with my father.

Living in the West

The difference from the West to the East was immediately apparent. On the train we saw cars from the window—private cars—Volkswagens. In East Germany there were none. Not everything was destroyed. Factories were still there, and I got a job working in a factory that produced things like tubes. I worked there from 1949 to 1952. For more information about our early years there, you can read my mother's memoirs where she talks a little more about that time.

Section 2: From Halberstadt to Ratingen

Wandervogel, FDJ, and Lapland

During those years, I joined a youth organization. When I say organization, that is already a misnomer. In 1912, there was the 100-year anniversary celebration of the defeat of Napoleon, with parties and drinking and so on. There was a group of young people who weren't interested in that. They had a meeting on a mountain, camping in tents, and made a manifesto. They called themselves Wandervogel (*vogel* means bird in German). They were in opposition to the older generation. Basically, they were saying that they were the youth and wanted to do their own thing and discover the world in their own way. They wanted a natural way of life. They weren't interested in drinking; the women didn't wear makeup. The movement was of course badly damaged because many of them were killed during the First World War. After the First World War, it started up again, but a little differently. My father was part of it. My mother too, but only indirectly. Then came the Nazis and they basically forced everyone to become part of the Hitler Youth. The Wandervogel didn't disappear; lots of people went underground. I read interesting stories about the history of the Wandervogel and one characteristic is that they were all young. *We* were all young. We tolerated no leader who was more than maybe two years older than ourselves. Everyone knew each other by their nicknames and not by real names, which made it difficult for the Gestapo to get very far in chasing people down, I read later on, because no one really knew who the other was. By the time I was old enough to be part of it, I joined them.

I was a little disadvantaged because I was a worker. Most others were in gymnasium, like my brother, Ekkehart. But a group of girls and boys met regularly in Ratingen. We sang European folk songs and enjoyed nature and camping in forests. That was our main thing. Every week we went somewhere and met and sang. When we had more time we hitchhiked and camped all over Europe. We went everywhere. I hitchhiked to the Black Forest, to Italy several times, to Rome, to France. More importantly, we went to Sweden and to Denmark, and just hitchhiked, enjoying nature. Our main wish was to be independent and develop our own identities.

There were some other elements to our time in the Wandervogel besides just travel and camping. We participated in reforestation efforts. We demonstrated for a united Europe. We tried to understand the Nazi period and what happened there. We were young and didn't know much about it, so we read. We taught each other. I think my brother, Ekkehart, became a political scientist because of his experience in the Wandervogel. Travel and camping were our main activities, but the other elements were important because it meant we became involved in a meeting with the FDJ.

The FDJ was an East German state organization. The full name was *Freie Deutsche Jugend* (Free German Youth). It was basically communist indoctrination, and young East Germans had to join. We had nothing to do with them except for this big meeting they held in Meissen and invited us to come to join. I think this was after Stalin's death in 1953. They thought that we were naïve, bourgeois, whatever. However, we had educated ourselves, and we knew what East Germany was like. We knew the ideology. We knew the problems youths had there.

What was interesting to me was that their behavior was very much like the Hitler Youth. For example, whereas we would sit in a group with a guitar and sing, they had a *fanfaren* (drum and bugle corps) and they played on the balcony of a church for everyone, followed by a big, organized meeting and so on.

We were a restless generation. This was true in East Germany too, but they had a limited future there and their government wanted to squash their concerns. On the stage there were several officers of the East German army, politicians, and a minister. They all made presentations and then they answered questions. But anyone could ask questions. We in the Wandervogel group were well prepared. I wasn't because I was not very articulate, but there were others, and we knew what the worries of the East German youth were. For example, there was a law against switching study topics when you were a student, so when you started in psychology, for example, you could not study another topic, you had to remain a psychology student. That was one worry they had. So, we asked questions. We were in the audience, but we didn't sit all together. One of us would ask, "What about this?" Another person would ask, "What about that?" The organizers got very angry, and we learned later that they had planned to evict us. But many East German students were there who were pleased that we raised the issues. We stayed in contact with some of the people we met in Meissen who were sympathetic to us. So, we had several of these kinds of events that made us united and one could say educated—not in a formal sense, but in just knowing what was going on.

When I went to Hanover for engineering school I made good friends there and I joined another group of the Wandervogel. With some in that group we went to Lapland. Lapland is the northern part of Finland. The people that live there are Laps; they are nomads. Six of us hitchhiked there over one summer. We had the idea of going to Kiel, near the Danish border, to see if we could get a ship to take us. We waited and waited and ended up splitting up into two groups and took different routes. As soon as we split up, my group got picked up by a ship. The other group ended up hitchhiking through Denmark. We had decided to meet high in north. We had no telephone but agreed to leave a letter in the post office of a certain town to try and coordinate where we'd meet up. Logistics were much harder before cell phones!

The ship took us to a tiny Swedish village, a harbor. We didn't know where we were. We had sea maps, but no land maps. We decided to look for a railroad track and follow that until we got to a train station. Then, we'd know where we were. We did that and hitchhiked the rest of the way to Lapland where we met up with the other three in our group. We got a ride on a delivery truck to an outpost of the Laps. From the outpost we kept walking into no-man's land.

It was fascinating. We came across a little hut where we could stay, but we didn't want to stay there. We wanted to continue to explore the area. Then we had a disagreement. There was a river we needed to cross; it was deep and ice cold. Two people said, "We'll walk up the river and find a place where we can cross." We lost them. There was no way to track them. The four of us continued on to a mountain. We had a tent called a kota, which you could say was generated from Laps. Like a pyramid, it had four sides and was open at the top in the center so you could make fire in the middle. We had four of these; they had one and we had the others. But we found a Lapish place where the Laps had come and built little shelters like tents, little huts not with proper walls but made with sticks of wood. So, we stayed in those. Then we went up the mountain and we made a big flag, and we hoped our friends would see it and come find us. They did and we were united again. It was a tricky trip. At some point I slipped, fell badly, and broke my tooth. We decided to stay there, but one of them came with me back to the station where we started and from there I got a ride to a doctor. I went back to my friends once my tooth was fixed.

I was lucky on that trip. The other tricky thing that happened was that I almost fell into a crevasse. We had come upon a gap between two mountains, so we had to go down one side and back up on the other side. But it turned out there was ice on the bottom. We had knapsacks—we were weighed down and not very mobile—and I was wearing lederhosen. I slipped on the ice and went down; I couldn't regain control. In front of me, there was an abyss, a crevasse that was probably 200 feet deep. I could have easily gone overboard, but luckily this glacier stopped about a foot before the end, where there was gravel and I could stop sliding. That saved me.

One of my friends was already halfway up the other side when this happened, but the other one saw it and said, "Klaus, how could you do this?" How could I do it? I didn't really want to! It would have been the end of me. (The oldest guy in this group later on emigrated to Canada and married someone in the lumber business. I knew he was in Halifax. Marge and I took a trip to Halifax much later and I decided I had to find him. I looked him up on the internet and I found him, but he had just died. It turned out that he was not at all in lumber but was a teacher of graphic arts, so we could have had a lot of things in common.)

What did we do for money on all these trips? I had saved some money from work and our parents must have given us something. We didn't need much. People were happy to pick up strangers for a long drive; it gave them someone to talk to. We heard stories about people's lives. People told us about their marriages and other things we knew nothing about. Also, no matter where we went, we got invited into families' homes for meals. One meal we were fed turned out to be frog legs. Two of the friends we were with were immediately sick when they found out. I always tell my students how much the cultural makes a difference as to the kind of food you can digest, and much of it is in your mind and in the language.

Yugoslavia

In addition to Lapland, I had always dreamed of taking a motorcycle trip to Yugoslavia. Yugoslavia was still at that time a communist country and closed off to tourism. I had an idea that I would buy a motorcycle and drive there but in the end Ekkehart and I hitchhiked. It was really an amazing exploration. We went to Belgrade and visited a big museum about Tito and how he united Yugoslavia. We met nice people, communists, along the way. From Belgrade we hitchhiked to a town that was central to a movie called Die Brücke (*The Bridge*). It was a German-Yugoslav co-production of the Second World War about a nurse and there is a famous bridge in Mostar where much of it took place. We wanted to see this bridge. After Mostar we hitchhiked to another area where they had not seen a German since the Second World War, so we didn't know how we would be received. We were told not to go there, that the people there were all murderers. But we went anyway, and when we got there, the people there said, "You came from where? What? You survived that?"

Section 3: Ulm, Princeton, and coming to Philadelphia

There was already hostility between different regions that turned into a terrible war much later. Today it's easier to get around that region as they've built big highways and have lots of tourists. Back then, we had to take the train a few times because no one would pick us up hitchhiking. We still managed to go to Sarajevo, Dubrovnik, and the mountains of Herzegovina in addition to Belgrade and Mostar.

The trip to Yugoslavia was the last big trip I made before heading to Ulm.

Engineering School and Work

When I wasn't hitchhiking and camping, I took evening courses in Düsseldorf to prepare myself to go to engineering school. In 1952, I went to study engineering in Hanover at the Staatliche Ingenieurschule Hannover, now Fachhochschule Hannover, two and a half years before I became a student in Ulm. The first thing I had to do was find a room to rent. It felt very third world. The landlady let me have one bath a week. She had a metal bathtub and she prepared warm water for it, but she was stingy and took a bath after I was done without changing the water.

The engineering education was normal. For my degree, I had to make a special project and actually I made something very innovative: I designed a steam engine for a car. It turned out to be like the Wankel engine. There was a gasoline-driven Wankel engine that had the same principle and I did mine before that. Mine wouldn't have worked, I know that, but it's one of the things I did in school. When I graduated, I got a job as an engineer in an engineering consulting firm in Düsseldorf and I commuted from Ratingen. I was the youngest person in the firm.

I had good ideas at this job, but they were not always received well. There was one particular incident that ended it for me at this firm. A company asked us to figure out a solution to a particular problem. Two of us went into the client's shop, talked to the people there, and developed a good idea as to what needed to be done. Separately, the boss went to the board and got a totally different idea. Now, whose idea counts? The boss's. I was very upset. I thought that was unethical and I wrote a letter saying as much. That was something that really upset me a lot.

In addition, thanks to the engineering school training, I was very competent and soon saw that I was more competent than those around me. I could calculate things better than my older colleagues and I had better ideas. I think I was not really fully given credit for it and not fully accepted. This letter I wrote was actually written in anticipation that I would be leaving anyway, and I resigned.

Section 2: From Halberstadt to Ratingen

A Krippendorff family event, before the war

The Krippendorffs (back row: Ekkehart, Lotte, Herbert, Klaus; front row: Rainer and Ute)

Klaus: A Memoir

Examples of Meissen porcelain. The small dish in the foreground is one of the few items not destroyed in the bombing of our home in Halberstadt.

A piece of Meissen porcelain that survived the war, along with one of Lotte's spoons

Section 3
Ulm, Princeton, and coming to Philadelphia

Hochschule für Gestaltung

I was not that satisfied as an engineer, and don't think a different engineering job would have made a difference. I thought engineering was too simple. I wanted a way to do something better, but I didn't know what.

There was a Wandervogel, Cornelia Koch, who was in a school in Ulm called *Hochschule für Gestaltung* (HfG), and she told me about the new ideas they were playing with. This interested me so I started to look into it. One of the motivations for me was that politically Ulm was kind of on my side, on the side of the youth movement. And it allowed me to move away from engineering, which was boring and not challenging enough. There was a discussion in our family: my parents said I shouldn't go there and I should focus on getting married. My wanting to go there was in opposition to my parents' imagination for my future. But two people supported me: my Tante Hilde and the daughter of Tante Dorle. I paid for everything myself, although in Germany you basically get free education.

The school had four departments: product design, architecture, graphics, and information. Information was a new concept: to think about design things, movies, writing. It was a very small department, but it was considered a bit of an elite department because it had the better teachers. The application form asked for all kinds of interesting things, not just to find out who you were and what you did in the past, but also things like which artists you preferred. They wanted to sort out people who were old-fashioned.

I was not really an artist and they didn't really say very much about this. But as an engineer I was attractive to them because they wanted to shift into more rational, functional, and scientific work. There was an idea of applying scientific issues to design, not just imagination, which had been their practice. They adopted me because of this idea; they protected and accepted me because I was an engineer. There were a few engineers in this school. They came from art schools and architecture schools, and lots of them came from Switzerland because a founder of the school, Max Bill, was a Swiss artist, designer, and theoretician. He was really the dominant character who gave the whole school kind of a new purpose.

One or two of the administrators came from Germany. One was Inge Scholl and the other one was her husband, Otl Aicher, who was a graphic artist. Inge Aicher-Scholl had two siblings who were executed in 1943 because they distributed anti-fascist leaflets as members of the White Rose student resistance group. They had been in the east war zone in Poland and had seen destruction and discrimination against the Jews. They formed a group that wrote notes and letters and distributed them widely. They sent their letters anonymously to different kinds of people, hoping they would get support or understanding. But they didn't really have any support, so that made it easier for them to get caught. At some point they distributed letters at the university in Munich, and they were caught by the building administrator. There was a movie made about the process after that; it was terrible for them. It was a famous case. Inge's sister's name, Sophie Scholl, is very famous in Germany, at least among our generation of people who were a little bit opposed to hierarchies.

Inge Aicher-Scholl was a major leader in the BDM (League of German Girls / *Bund Deutscher Mädel*) in Ulm. She was kind of the top woman of all the other organizations underneath her. The siblings who were caught hadn't wanted to talk to her, so there was no communication between them because they knew Inge was on the wrong side. At the time the siblings were caught, there was a law in Germany whereby the whole family was responsible for each individual member. That meant her father, Robert Scholl, who was a tax consultant and had lots of clients from the Nazi party, was put in prison. So was Inge. But she wasn't a major leader in the White Rose, so she was privileged by every means. Afterward, people had looked for documents of Gestapo interviews and couldn't find any, and that struck me as suspicious. When the war ended, she played victim of the Nazi regime. Because she had been in jail, she could say, "They threw me in jail." She wrote a book about her brother and sister called *Die Weiße Rose*. She did not mention any of the other people involved; it was very, very strange.

Now, I didn't know all of that when I went to the school, but I knew *Die Weiße Rose* and admired those two people who were killed. I knew of the siblings, a brother in particular, when I went to Ulm because one of them was actually in the Wandervogel. When the Wandervogel

Section 3: Ulm, Princeton, and coming to Philadelphia

was converted into Hitler Youth, this brother maintained some of the songs and so on, and he was a leader. That was not acceptable, so he was not promoted under the Nazi regime. The school was initially thought of being named for the two siblings. Inge Aicher-Scholl, now anti-fascist, got lots of money from the United States at that time to build that school in the name of her siblings.

It was only after Inge Aicher-Scholl got connected to Max Bill that the concept of a graphics and design school came about. He argued that German industry was so demolished that they had to develop a new culture that was totally different than a Germanic Nazi kind of culture and rebuild based on this new culture. This school was very much organized around the idea of doing things differently. That was very appealing to me. I'd visited once before with this girl from Wandervogel and saw a very impressive exhibition of their work. That's why I decided to join.

There were buildings just off the HfG campus for students to live, but not enough, so the first-year students had to live in Ulm. I lived with two other HfG students. Our landlady told me that Inge Aicher-Scholl was the most brutal leader in Ulm. Everyone despised her. To my regret still, I never talked to Inge Aicher-Scholl, whom I met many times, about her past and how she made this transition. We were so involved in design that these sad comments were not really that important at the time.

Later on, there was a German person who'd immigrated to the United States and then went back to Germany to study. She wanted to see all the other people that were involved in this White Rose thing. She interviewed them and wrote something about it. I was in communication with her, and she told me many other stories I didn't know. Inge had a diary during the whole Nazi period. At some point apparently, Hitler came with a car while she was walking with her group of girls and she managed to stop him and talk to him. That was kind of why she was important. When I went to Ulm and heard these stories, I registered them and was not really that interested, but later on, it became very clear that was something that I would have liked to know more about. Maybe Inge wasn't genuine. I just don't know.

The First Year

I started in the fall of 1956. I wouldn't say this school billed itself as an avant-garde school, but it was that in every way because designers and design teachers are people who often think about the future. The school invited all kinds of people to lecture who were ahead of their time, including people from the United States. For example, before I was there, Norbert Wiener, the inventor of cybernetics, was invited to give a talk. I don't know what people understood from it, but we were exposed to totally new ways of thinking. That was very exciting to me. There were other people invited from the United States and there were many returning emigrants—people who had emigrated to the United States and Sweden, but came back to Germany. One of the returning emigrants was a teacher that I admired, a sociologist or cultural anthropologist, who taught courses about cultural anthropology with the framework of design, objects, and how one relates to technology.

Design was important, but the framework was the thing that excited me. There was a philosopher from Stuttgart close by, and he got hold of a book on information theory, a mathematical theory developed during the war but published only in 1949. It was an important piece of thinking that made communication a discipline because he quantified information and tried to make it a science. In the United States, for example, there was journalism education, but they focused on writing. Then that was superseded by radio and television, for which there was no education. So, journalism had to move in that direction but they still mainly focused on writing. There was one man who wanted to make a communications department in Iowa, but he was not allowed to do that because it was somehow not acceptable to journalists. Then he went to the University of Illinois, where he was the head of the University of Illinois press, and he went there only with the promise that he could open a Department of Communications. The information theory was kind of a justification. The idea was that there is a science behind communication, and not just writing.

Klaus as a student

In Ulm, there was a philosophy professor in the information science department who did everything in terms of information. He wrote many books and introduced totally different ways of thinking. He said—correctly, I think—that, for example, avant-garde poets

Section 3: Ulm, Princeton, and coming to Philadelphia

are generally not accepted and it's only after some time that people start realizing there is something that the poets have to say. He explained it in terms of information: when something has too much information, you don't get it. It's only slowly that you can learn it, and then you get it. That was kind of his framework, the more culturally informed, mathematical philosophy.

I chose product design as my focus. This was kind of close to my background, but I was always more general. I had to be in one department but I did many other things. I have to say that the first year was really revolutionary. The first year was meant to streamline everyone about the general idea of design and the principles. The idea was that one should break down everyone's different ideas of art and design so they were focused on the problems of design in various areas. Everyone had to do things like painting, designing types, typography, designing spaces, and making models. Then you went into one of the four departments. We had graphic artists presenting things. There was one woman, Helene Nonne-Schmidt, who was from the Bauhaus in Dessau before it was closed by the Nazis. She taught color, and I still have some paintings and things that I made in her class. We took typography. At the end of the year, one teacher gave us an assignment involving painting very small squares. Computers make that so easy today, but at that time, we did it by hand. It was a boring exercise, painting hundreds of little squares about maybe half an inch size, and very precisely. Recently someone reminded me that one guy, a graphic artist and typographer, assigned us a project of making a computer-readable type. We didn't have computers yet, but he knew already it would be needed. We were on the edge of almost everything.

Political Involvement

The Russians had invaded Hungary around the same time that I started school at Ulm. The Austrians were overwhelmed by an amazing number of refugees and could not cope. It was all in disarray. Some people from the Wandervogel suggested we go there and help. My brother Ekkehart went there at some point, and I convinced all the first-years to go shortly before Christmas; it was basically Christmas break. The director of the school—actually, the one who gave us the square assignment, Maldonado—said we couldn't go so the number of people who went was reduced to only four: one American and three Germans. We—Nick Chaparos, Bernd Meurer, Werner Kilian,

Hermann Edel, and I—drove to Austria in Nick's Volkswagen. We couldn't do very much because around the same time, shortly before that, there was an American who had ferried people from one side of the river to the other in his boat. But he didn't know that the other side, which he thought was Austrian, belonged to Hungary, too. The Russians came and arrested him, which created a lot of problems for the Austrian government and who consequently forbade foreigners from going to the border.

There was an amazing number of people who tried to help. When the refugees came over, they didn't know whether they were in Austria or not. This resonated with me coming from East Germany to West Germany. They didn't know where they were and they would hide if they saw a car coming, so as not to be caught. The people helping had to basically catch them and tell them they were safe. That's something I thought we would help do, but we were prevented from this and had to help in the cafeteria instead, where a Swiss hotel chef had come to help. I met an amazing number of people. In the end, we thought that helping in a cafeteria was really not something where we were useful in the way we wanted to be, so we looked for other opportunities.

Next, we went to Vienna and met someone who was in charge of a princess; we wanted to talk to her and recruit her to help. We were told that she was involved in a ball and she couldn't talk to us. She was in a totally different world. We had to give that idea up.

In Vienna we didn't have anywhere to sleep. I remembered from my trip to Sweden that when we couldn't find a place to sleep, we'd gone to the police and asked if we could sleep in the prison. I suggested that we do that now. We went to the Austrian police, but they had, of course, never heard of young people wanting to sleep in prison. Here came these four foreigners and they wanted to be in prison for a day, for a night's sleep. Also, we were odd people. One was an artist, and the American didn't understand much of Austrian history. In the police station, he saw a picture of a strange character and asked who it was. It was a former king of Austria and the police officer was offended because the American was dismissive of that, so there was lots of tension. Around midnight, they finally let us sleep in the prison and we had to get all our pockets emptied, just like regular prisoners. We were in this prison cell going through corridors, just like in a movie. I think we only got three hours of sleep. When the cleaning people came, all of whom were prisoners, they asked us what we did to be in there. We got something to eat, a chunk of bread and some coffee. It was terrible. But overall, it was a good experience. And then we went home to Ulm and had a big accident on the autobahn, but that's another issue.

After this first year, I was elected student representative for my department. Like me, there were many students who wanted to see some changes made in the way the school was run. For instance, the design teachers usually had jobs in the industry. This was fine because it kept them real and not just theoretical, but I thought they neglected their teaching as a result. Their jobs became more important. We started to complain to the administration about this, and I was one of the student representatives who did so.

One of my fellow students who wasn't in product design and later became a therapist, said, "Klaus, you argue too quickly. Here's a pipe; take a puff before you answer." He was right. Much later, one of my heroes in the area of poetry and theater was Bertolt Brecht. He was an immigrant from Germany and kind of a communist. He testified in front of the House Committee on Un-American Activities, and I have the record of his hearing. Someone said in English, "Did you write this poem?" He showed Brecht the poem and Brecht said, "There's no answer." They pressed him: "Did you write this poem or not?" He said, "I wrote the German poem." Later on, I found out that he was smoking a cigar, and he took a few puffs before answering. I smoked for maybe ten years afterward, but only socially and only a pipe. I never inhaled, so I was not really an addicted smoker. There's something good about not responding quickly and thinking about it. My parents did not smoke. It was part of the Wandervogel culture not to smoke or anything like that; we were natural. The idea of being natural and exploring nature was a solid philosophy and I carry it even now, I think.

We survived the first year. It introduced us to architecture, to all kinds of things. But the most important parts of my experiences were really the lectures and opening up to different areas of thought. Engineering education is very specialized, very narrow. Ulm was the opposite.

Homing In on Important Ideas

At some point, one of the professors resigned and they hired a young mathematician, Horst Rittel, to teach information theory in his place. I went to his first lecture. He was not a philosopher, and he developed all the probability theories on the blackboard.

People just didn't understand it. But he was very flexible, adjusting and understanding what design is about. He developed all kinds of interesting theories, saying, for example, that design is planning. Design means not just making a project and saying you produced it, but you have to plan where it goes, for whom, and so on. He also introduced us to all kinds of mathematical issues, like systems theory: the idea that one should think of a product as part of a larger complex system. When you design a fuse, then you have to know what the whole system of electricity is about. And then came cybernetics. Cybernetics is a science dealing with circularity and feedback. You have to keep learning. When you design a product, you ought to look at how it's being used, and that should teach you to do the next thing better. That is the very simplistic idea of cybernetics.

This professor was really an amazing character. He turned out to be only three years older than me, but he had a university education and later on he went to Berkeley and became very important in many ways. He introduced so many different ideas to us, ideas I grew up on.

In the summer, I had nothing to do when school was out. One summer I worked in a factory's design department in Ulm. At some point I went to England because my English was miserable and I thought I had to learn it. Through a connection, I went through a design department in Oxford, and they helped me get room and board for three months. But I didn't learn any English because designers draw, they don't argue. The people I lived with were Irish workmen; there was no communication. But at least I was in England.

I went to a bookstore there, Blackwell, the famous publishing house. I bought two books. One was by Ross Ashby, *An Introduction to Cybernetics,* because I thought that this was something I needed to learn more about. This book was published in 1956 and I was there around 1958. I thought that was important, and my mathematician professor knew of him and had mentioned him at times. The other book I bought was Ludwig Wittgenstein's *Tractatus Logicus Philosophicus.* Ludwig Wittgenstein was an Austrian aristocrat. Before the First World War, he studied in England under Bertrand Russell, the famous philosopher. Then came the First World War and he was drafted by the Austrian army and became a prisoner of war of the British. During his time as a prisoner, he finished his doctoral dissertation and asked a British soldier to take it to Bertrand Russell in England. After the First World War, he just gave up on philosophy and became a schoolteacher, but then realized that was also not for him. He asked Bertrand Russell whether he could come there, and he got a professorship in Oxford. But he was German and his English was probably not very good. He wrote this *Tractatus* in German, and it was translated. The book has one page in German, one page in English. I thought that was something I could learn English from. But it was ridiculous because it was philosophy. I did not learn from him; it was a naive conception. However, Wittgenstein later became of extreme importance to me because he was against the traditional notion of language as being always about things. Language had something to do with how one organizes one's life. He said that meaning is not what you have in mind or what it is, meaning has to do with the response you get. Well, that was revolutionary. In many ways, much later, I have really appreciated him. And this book I bought was his first book and was not even so decisive. It's really a strange coincidence. These two people were very important to me later on.

Back at Ulm we had two big assignments that we had to complete: we had to design a product or prove our design ability and justify every step we took and write a theoretical analysis of something, like a thesis. Diploma work had a practical and theoretical aspect. For the practical work, I took on something that nobody had done before: I made a steel grader, which is a sort of plow. There's a cabin and a big engine, and from the cabin you can see the plow to adjust it. This is used for in planning, like making a new street. The challenge was to give the driver maximum control, viewing what he's doing and getting rid of certain things. And there was an esthetic element, of course. In Oxford, I'd gone to a company that made them, and they gave me everything that I needed to design one, though in the end they didn't really adopt it. However, it was the biggest object that was ever designed in Ulm. For that, I got an award for the best design from the German industry.

As for the theoretical work, I was let into the program because I was already an accomplished engineer, but I was bored with that. I was looking for the more complicated phenomena where human beings are involved. That's what I thought the school would do, but they were trying to get away from art and focused on functional design. That was very much like engineering, and I was never really so keen on that. I was more interested in social perception, with how human beings interact with devices.

Tomas Maldonado, the professor who was in charge of the school at some point, introduced an advanced topic: semiotics, the theory of signs. There is a very traditional notion of semiotics, that an idea is already a sign and that it has a reference. You analyze how the reference becomes a sign and it helps you recognize the sign. He taught that largely with graphic artists, which makes sense. I thought one should change to the direction of product design, not just making design objects like engineers, which I knew so well, but to look at design as an issue of communication, like this book. Yes, it needs to be written. That is the function. But the function is really not so important. It has to look nice, be used easily, put in your pocket, etc. So, I thought these were all communication issues and sign issues: that you recognize what you can use it for, not that you use it. I wanted to write about that.

I went to Maldonado and he said, "Klaus, you're mistaken. Objects are references, not signs." Since I fundamentally disagreed with him, I knew I could not work with him; instead, I went to Horst Rittle and he became my advisor. I wrote my thesis on the sign characteristics of objects: what one can learn from how they appear, how one can handle them, etc. That was actually a revolutionary idea. Later on, it would turn out to be a major thing in my own development and others'.

At the same time, after about four years, I worked with an American professor who was interested in perception. He wanted to make an Institute of Perception in Ulm, and I worked there as a research assistant. He came from Princeton and had been working with some perception theorists. They made demonstrations that perception is not just like a camera, taking pictures in your mind; it had something to do with history, with one's own philosophy. One of the things he always said in experiments was that a dollar was big to a poor person and small to rich one. The perception of the dollar changes quite radically. Later on, I made many more discoveries, and in fact, I wrote not about the size of the dollar but about how perception changes with the metaphors we use. I'm currently working on that. I didn't know anything about metaphors and language at that time. Perception was the issue.

That was a schism in the school. For example, the husband of Inge Aicher-Scholl, the graphic artist Otl Aicher, was very successful; I liked everything he did. But his position was that he didn't want to hear from us about color, that he knew everything. In my own mind I thought, *You know what to do, but you don't know what other people see.* And that is correct. One has to investigate not just one's own doing, but if you want to do something for other people, you have to know how other people think and what other people perceive. That was the gist of my thesis, that perception has something to do with what you want to do with something you see, particularly the design characteristics of that object.

I had three sometimes non-overlapping interests: design, cybernetics, and communication. I had all these ideas of moving away from an engineering approach and toward a human-centered design approach. I said that engineers made something that functions, but designers had to think of what it meant in terms of communication: how humans communicate with it, the interface design, how other people talk about using it, instructions as to how to use it...these points are also communication but not ever treated by engineers.

I also wrote a paper in a student journal we founded about engineers versus designers. I said that engineers deal with functions—it's simplistic, yes—but designers deal with communication. Maybe it was a little too radical, but I wanted to make a point. I was not so clear at that time, but take the function of an object for example. What is a function? Well of course, when you have a screwdriver, the function is to drive the screw, but you use the screwdriver for so many other things, like prying things open. If you focus only on the function, you eliminate options. I said that functions are always determined by an authority. You're given the function, and you have to comply in what you produce. But designers ought to be able to move away from that by considering what is important and the resulting changes. That was my objection to the Ulm philosophy.

My objections aside, Ulm was transformational mainly because of the ideas that were presented. The school became very famous and everyone adopted their curriculum and ideas. I remained friends with many from Ulm. At some point in 1968 or even before that, there were problems funding the school because it was actually a private foundation and they also required government support. They were, one could say, a bit arrogant because they looked down on everyone else; that didn't go well with some politicians and they cut down the funding. At some point there was a very low level of funding. I was already out by then. But because they were kind of revolutionary, I was asked whether I would come there as a teacher after I'd left. They invited me to go there and give a lecture several times, which I did. It was interesting to see old faces and offer different perspectives, now from the outside.

The school didn't live; avant-garde schools never live long. It closed in 1968.

Coming to the United States

In September 1961 I came by boat to the United States on the steamship *Bremen,* on a Fulbright Travel Grant and a Ford

International Fellowship. It was a ten-day trip to cross the Atlantic. I think nowadays, why feed someone on a ship for ten days instead of flying them and giving them one lunch or something? People got seasick during the trip. I was in a small group of about eight in one cabin and we decided not to get seasick, and it worked. Many people didn't go to lunch because they were seasick, so we'd sit around a table at lunchtime and laugh about everyone else. I met many interesting people on the ship. There was one artist who was supposed to be in America for a year and showed his art to everyone. We later became good friends and traveled to universities together; he went to Temple University's art department and was there while I was at Princeton.

My first experience in the U.S. was New York Harbor, which was miserable and rundown. There was a big street overrun with cars driving by, and I was surprised how many of them were damaged. I thought, *What kind of country is this?* In Germany, when there is a crack, you repair it immediately; in the United States, you're driving as long as it doesn't fall apart. My brother Ekkehart picked me up in New York. He'd been there for two years already; he'd gotten a fellowship and was at Columbia University. One of the nice things he did was bring me to the outside of an old castle or something, overlooking Manhattan, just to introduce me to the United States. We had a long discussion of what it meant to be in the U.S., to be a student, and that was really important. I stayed at his place and from there I had some of my first experiences in New York.

To meet a friend who was in New York, I went on the subway for the first time and then on a bus. I was robbed because I had 400 German marks that I'd exchanged into dollars on the ship. I didn't really know how American dollars looked, so I was looking at them on the bus. Someone must have seen me, and when I walked out, they pushed me and suddenly my pocket was empty and I had no money. When I'd gotten my

A sample of the masks Klaus collected

award in Germany for the best design, I'd received some money, and I bought a Volkswagen in Germany and brought it to the U.S. I was parked in front of my brother's house and I didn't think that someone would break into the car, but they did. They took my camera and lots of other things. I was slowly learning what life was like here.

I also went to museums, like the Museum of Natural History. This is where I first saw masks. I was fascinated and developed a lifelong interest in them as a result.

Searching for Schools

Now I had to face the issue of where to study. There was the Institute of International Education in New York, which looked at your background and mission and found a place for you. They didn't know about this oddball Krippendorff who had so many ideas and wanted to study subjects for which there was no department: cybernetic systems theory, game theory, all of these things. But I had a recommendation from an American professor, Bud Perrine, who had recently graduated from Princeton in social psychology. It was a glowing recommendation and because of that they suggested I go to Princeton. It made sense from their point of view, and so I went.

Lots of things surprised me about life at Princeton. I went to register for classes, and at that time my English was pretty bad, but I managed. There was only one woman at the school, and she was Indian. I didn't know that it had been entirely a men's university and had only fairly recently started accepting women.

There was a big pool where men were naked. It was unheard of for me. There were so many things like that that were odd. I knew nothing about American football, but I went to a game between Princeton and Harvard. It had been raining and the Princetonians used toilet paper to make signs on the street for Princeton to win. They allowed me to be a photographer and I took lots of pictures of the football games. I didn't even know what photos I should take, but it was certainly interesting.

There was another German student who wanted to us to move in together, but I wanted to live with Americans; I wanted to learn English. I managed to make friends in the psychology department. There were three Americans who were looking for a fourth and I was the one. They were very different from me and one another. The most outstanding one was tall, rich, and drove a Porsche. He had parties and invited lots of girls. His greatest pleasure was when they were all there, he went to his room where he had a boa constrictor in a cage, and wrapped it around himself. All the girls would start screaming, "Ahh!" I didn't have very much contact with the second American, but the third one took me to a festivity that I had never heard of: Thanksgiving. His parents lived in Idaho or somewhere, and we drove all the way. For the first time I was with an American family and learned about Thanksgiving.

The most important thing about my time at Princeton was that I was a misfit intellectually. I couldn't defend my arguments very well because my English was bad. I started out copying lecture notes in German until I realized this was not the way to learn it, then I changed to English. I learned English from living, not like you normally learn, from books and translation. My roommates were great. They brought me to do things like go shopping and basically introduced me to ordinary living in the United States. That's where I learned my English—not enough, but a start at least.

Princeton had changed since I first met the professor in Ulm, Perrine, who had studied there and who had written my recommendation letter. He had studied social psychology at Princeton and the social part had since been minimized because they'd only kept one professor with that interest. The other ones were rat psychologists. I had to learn mathematical theory or learning theory for rats. This was so far removed from what I wanted to do, but because this fellowship was relatively new, there was an article to be written about me coming to Princeton with photos of me, and published in *The Daily Princetonian*. I wrote the photo caption, "Here comes the German psychologist studying American rats." When I wrote that, I knew this was not for me.

I felt totally lost. Hadley Cantrell was the former chair of the psychology department and had retired. He was very much acquainted with the professor I'd met who gave me this recommendation. I went to him and said it wasn't working. He agreed it was not the right place for me. He knew some people, so he gave me several names of people to visit at MIT, Harvard, the University of Michigan, and the University of Illinois, to which I added once I was in Michigan, Michigan State University. When I traveled to other schools from Princeton, I was looking for a place to go. I came from this design school and had these half-cooked ideas of cybernetics, information theory, planning, game theory, social perception. I was looking for whoever could help me know more about these things. Princeton was definitely not it.

Section 3: Ulm, Princeton, and coming to Philadelphia

The people I met on this trip were very important and I only talked to each of them for maybe half an hour. George A. Miller at MIT was an information theorist, and his most famous paper is about the magical number seven, plus or minus two. That means you cannot think of more than seven things, plus or minus two. When you have, say, a questionnaire, if you have more than seven questions, plus or minus two, then it is too much. You cannot think about more than seven at a time. That was his bag. I met Jerome Bruner from Harvard (the famous educational philosopher who made major contributions in education and communication); Anatol Rapaport at the University of Michigan; and George Gerbner, who later became the dean at Annenberg. At Michigan State, where I knew some Ulmerts who had gotten their PhD, I had a more in-depth interview. I met Hans Toch and David Berlo there. Berlo was the head of the communications department, and he threw a party where I was essentially being interviewed but didn't realize it—at the end of which I was given an assistantship, which was totally unheard of. I was definitely naive as far as communication is concerned, but they wanted me. They were the ones who pointed out that I should try the University of Illinois with George Gerbner. I was mainly enthused about Illinois because of Ross Ashby and the cybernetics angle, so that's where I went next.

I talked to the department head there who was a very pro-European scholar; he told me lots of things that interested me and it seemed very pleasant. I went to talk to the head of the design department, and it was a miserable department, very low-level in comparison with Ulm. He was actually more interested in interviewing me. When I mentioned cybernetics, he said they had a cybernetician there, whom he introduced me to. The cybernetician was Austrian originally and really outgoing, and he greeted me almost as if I were an old friend. When I told him what I had been doing and what I wanted to do, he said they had a course there in cybernetics. It was taught by Ross Ashby, the one whose book I bought. That's when I knew Illinois was it.

I was there for only two and a half years. The University of Illinois looked at my record and thought, *He must be fake. He comes from a school for which we don't have a degree. He comes to Illinois from Princeton. Who would do that?* They let me enroll as an undergrad, and I got all As and was invited to many honors fraternities. I didn't even know what these fraternities were about. I joined none. All this new vocabulary and culture were obstacles that I had to master. There are even more obstacles if you don't fall in a traditional track, which I didn't. But I think I learned to manage them. For example, I didn't come to the United States to get a PhD. I wanted to just grow the ideas that were planted in me in Ulm. I wanted to get more information and understand them. But at University of Illinois they said, "You can't just take courses. You have to be a PhD candidate." So, I learned how the American system worked and became a PhD candidate.

The department of education was very interdisciplinary. People from sociology, psychology, social psychology, anthropology, linguistics, and economics were all part of the faculty. In fact, my advisor in the end was a linguist. I could take Ashby's course too, and Ashby was probably the most influential teacher to me. It was a one-year course. I was still working with a cybernetician on cybernetics and I advanced the notion in many ways. I was the first person from the communications department to ever take this course. After that, several other people followed, and my advisor saw the virtue of it and sent others. This was really a very open department. I learned about mass communication, which was kind of boring, but it taught me a lot about the things I had to do later.

I explored many different topics there, but the courses that interested me most besides Ashby's cybernetics were cultural anthropology, linguistics, and linguistic anthropology. In the anthropology course, we learned about different arts and we were given the assignment to look into different kinds of kinship terms in different cultures. Everyone had a different culture and literature. I realized that when you came to a country as a foreigner, you used your own criteria as an anthropologist to understand what was around you. All of these things we learned and explored were really eye-opening.

Then came an important moment. I was working with two professors, coding transcripts. There was a young professor, psychologist Shell Feldman, and George Gerbner, who was a more established person. I took a course of Gerbner's and hated it because I had to learn the formulas of how to see things. He was teaching mass communication. He had a degree in education from the University of Southern California, but he specialized in communication and was driven by saying, "Mass communication in the United States is really an industry. Money is the issue, making profit the issue." This was all true, but it was not enough in my opinion. Meanwhile, Walter Annenberg paid for the creation of the University of Pennsylvania's school of communication with the misconception that the Annenberg School would train journalists to work at *The Inquirer,* which he owned. The university said they couldn't do that kind of thing, but Gilbert Seldes apparently appeased Walter Annenberg, saying they would do it, but not so narrowly. There was a photography department, a graphics department, a radio department, and a television studio, and that made no real sense. Then he retired, and a temporary dean was there while they looked for a new dean. They offered the post to the chief of the University of Illinois' communication department, Charles Osgood. He said no. They asked George Gerbner, who was very ambitious, and he was interested. He asked Charles Osgood to nominate him, and he was interviewed and was made dean of Annenberg. Then there was this other young character who independently applied to become a member of the faculty. I actually took a ride with him from Illinois to Philadelphia, where I was also interviewed by the dean. I must have left a good impression, but the new dean, George Gerbner, was already hired.

Coming to Philadelphia and the Annenberg School of Communication

I came to Philadelphia in 1964, but I didn't have my PhD at that time. I had finished my coursework and my qualifying examination and was about to write my dissertation. I gave them, I think, three proposals. I forgot one, but the other that I didn't do was to look at how communication structures get subverted by totalitarian regimes. I was thinking of Nazi Germany, but my model was the Incas: the Incas had fantastic roads and all of them went to the city center. The Spanish came and could travel these roads and because they were taken to be gods by the Incas, they were received well, took the gold from the center, and then kept Mexico as a colony. I didn't choose this option in the end because I would have had to go to South America and learn Spanish and that was too much.

For my dissertation, I chose content analysis, mainly because this methodology was kind of underdeveloped; the field of communications didn't really have many good analytical methods. People had very simplistic notions of it. There were two basic ideas that are uniquely related to communication. One is network analysis: the idea that communication is not just from A to B but creates complicated networks. The other one is, what is communicating? I wrote my dissertation with one chapter for almost every member of faculty I studied with: one on cybernetics, information theory, anthropology, etc. My approach was to make a more general methodology that would be appropriate to many situations.

Getting my PhD was much more complicated because I had a J4 visa and it required that after my studies in the U.S. I should have left the country for two years before I could re-enter. But I had been hired at the Annenberg School and I thought that was better for me than returning to Germany. If I finished my dissertation, I would have been immediately sent back out of the country. I got a very good letter from George Gerber about my importance in the field as part of his effort to lobby various authorities to keep me in the country. He wrote that everything around me would fall to pieces if I left.

The point is, I could not leave for a while and I had to delay getting my dissertation. While I was in Philadelphia, I worked on my dissertation and delayed submission until I could get rid of this J4 issue. I'd already started my career at Penn while I was a research assistant; I taught a class on content analysis but was called a research assistant. My salary was $6,000 a year.

Section 4

Marriage and Children

Meeting Sultana

I first saw Sultana in the Communications Library at Urbana. She was a student there too, an English major who was seven years younger than me. She worked in the library and we got to talking. We were both foreign students so when there was an event of the Foreign Students Association, I asked if she wanted to go. We went together but the problem was that she couldn't dance. The event was largely a dancing thing, but since she didn't dance it meant that we could sit together and just chat. I learned that she was from East Pakistan, from Dhaka. Sultana's whole family had fled in 1948 from India to East Pakistan since they were Muslims (though she was far from religious), and she came to the United States through a Rotarian Fellowship. I was very impressed. What I found fascinating was that she was at the so-called marrying age in East Pakistan, which meant your relatives found a husband for you. She wanted to escape that. I found that very encouraging, and besides, she was intelligent.

At some point, I wanted to take a spring vacation with a student from Italy to explore the South in my Volkswagen. We mentioned that to Sultana, and she said she wanted to come with us. It was the South of a kind that I had no experiences with. For example, we saw a restaurant on a street corner that we wanted to go into. It had two entrances, one on each side of the corner. We walked in one entrance without thinking about it. Some

Sultana and Klaus

Black people came up to the same entrance and the people at the restaurant said they had to go through a second entrance we hadn't seen. Even though we had gone through the main entrance we still had a problem because Sultana was not exactly white and she wore a sari. Nobody objected verbally, but slowly people started to walk out. None of us had ever experienced something like that. And there were many "Whites Only" signs everywhere. This was in '62 and it was shocking.

After dinner we had to find a place to sleep and we went to a motel. The room had two beds and we were three people. There came a moment where Sultana was sitting on the table but was sleepy and almost fell asleep on the table. I thought that was horrible. I had a sleeping bag and could sleep on the floor, so I picked her up and brought her to one of the beds. I think at that point something clicked. On the drive back to Urbana, we held hands, even though I was driving and it was dangerous. I hadn't really thought initially that she was a prospect for me, but I was increasingly fascinated by her story and her background.

She came to see me occasionally in the small room I was living in on top of the Quaker Center, and at some point she told me that her sociology professor made sexual advances toward her but she managed to get out of it. I had never heard of such a thing, that a professor would do that. I knew that professor well because he was teaching in the communications department. I consoled her, and we became increasingly close.

In my last year, a friend of mine who was also from the communication department was looking for a roommate and I thought he would be a good fit, so I moved in. Next door was another student from a different department and she wanted a roommate too, so Sultana moved in with her. We were very close physically and we spent more and more time together. When I first met Sultana, she was an English major, which she had also studied in East Pakistan, but she hated it and shifted to communications. Maybe it was me, maybe it was working in the communications library, but she was increasingly fascinated with communications. We had a lot of things in common.

There weren't many other Pakistani people in town, but there was one family from East Pakistan, a couple with a child, whom she knew. I spent a lot of time with her and that family. I got kind of acclimated to that culture and I think that brought me closer to Sultana as well. We spent lots of time cooking together. We appreciated each other a lot and we did a lot of things together. In Urbana, it was mostly movies. Urbana was a very interesting place because it was an island in the middle of nowhere. But the advantage of Urbana was they were very conscious of being so isolated. They had new movies as soon as they came to New York. As soon as there were theater performances, they had them. Culturally, we were pretty much up to date.

In 1964, I was hired at the University of Pennsylvania. Sultana came with me when I drove to do the interview, and we looked for an apartment. We were basically a couple of sorts, although she had to go back to Urbana to finish her coursework. In the summer of '65, she took a job in New York and lived with my brother Ekkehart and my sister-in-law Eve before she got her own apartment. I thought they gelled very well. The four of us went camping together once in '65, and then we went constantly back and forth between the University of Pennsylvania and Urbana. I drove several times to Urbana. It was a long thirteen-hour drive, but I did it.

On December 30, 1965, we got married. A friend of mine managed the Christian ceremony in the church—he was a communications student who was also a Christian minister—I forget which denomination. Another acquaintance of Sultana's who was Muslim organized the Muslim ceremony the next day. All our professors and many students came. One couple loaned us a house to have a big party. It was very, very nice. My parents came to the wedding, but her parents did not.

When Sultana had her coursework nearly finished but had not written her dissertation, she came to Philadelphia and lived with me. We lived on the 3600 block of Baring Street. We socialized in many ways: we invited lots of people from Penn over, and she had some friends from Pakistan. Around 1966, a Pakistani friend of hers visited, Sharifa Berm, who was slightly older than Sultana. She started first in East Pakistan, then went to the American University in Beirut and had married a German mathematician professor.

We talked about the difficulties of why her parents were not really accepting our marriage. We had no idea why. Then we thought we should give a call to East Pakistan. This was complicated at that time because there was a landline to England, but from England to East Pakistan, communication had to be by a radio, which was very unreliable and had to be scheduled.

At the time, Sultana's family had fled India; the way it worked for many people was that you made an agreement with someone Hindu in Pakistan who wanted to go to India, and you exchanged property with them. Sultana's family had a big house in India and built another one in East Pakistan. Sultana's father was an English-educated orthopedic surgeon and had lots of clients. He was apparently very much liked and had contacts with the post office, so the post office men came to his house to be sure that the radio/phone connection was working in the new house. It turned out to be a long process, and apparently all the relatives came to the new house and were sitting in a circle, waiting to be part of this call with us.

I didn't know with whom I was talking when I first got on the phone. My problem was that I started the call by just saying "hello?" but the British operator told me we had to speak in full sentences in order to connect to Sultana's family over the phone. It was difficult. But after I spoke in full sentences and we were connected to her family, my wife took over and was able to talk to almost everyone on the other end.

Visiting East Pakistan

Sultana had a sister who was two years younger, Najma, who was about to be married (it was an arranged marriage). She was told by an aunt that you never tell anyone you are about to be married. That was an important rule. But the sister dared to disobey and asked Sultana to come to the wedding. That was a big violation of this family tradition.

Now, the aunt, we found out later, had two young daughters. She was sure that if there was a foreigner marrying into the family, her daughters would never get married because no one wanted to be married to someone who had a foreigner in their family. I don't know what image they had of a foreigner. Maybe they thought I was a cowboy, gun-slinging type...I had no idea. Later on, there were other indications of prejudices that existed among that family. Sultana's grandmother was bedridden and about to die but did not know that Sultana married a foreigner. She was told, and then she said, "Oh my God. All the children will be Black." I don't know if that is the same prejudice the aunt had, but the aunt was definitely hostile to the whole idea of who I was, as an outsider.

The aunt did everything possible to move up the date so that when we would come, the marriage would already be complete. I don't know why Sultana's parents had nothing to say in this matter. It was really the aunt's business for some reason. But the father of the groom was a very devoted Muslim and he consulted the stars. He found that it was not a good idea to change the wedding to an earlier date because there were some bad omens. The wedding date stayed the same as they had initially agreed.

Around 1965, my brother Rainer had gone on something like a student exchange to Masada in Israel to help with excavations as a summer job. Then he continued hitchhiking to India, where a friend of his needed help. Rainer was hired to visit various Gandhian villages and report on things like how and what they were doing economically. He spent almost a year in India, traveling around.

When Rainer heard that we had this conversation with Sultana's family, he decided to leave India and go to East Pakistan. That was very uncertain for me. Should one do it? But he was a very social person and I was sure he would do the best one can do, so he went there. It turned out that he was very much appreciated by Sultana's family and was curious about so many things; he was acquainted with Indian food, with Indian everything. He spent about ten days there with the family. He ended up meeting Sultana's family before I did.

Then he hitchhiked back from East Pakistan to Germany. Nowadays that goes through Afghanistan. He had with him a piece of gold jewelry for my mother from Sultana's family, a square brooch; the family was apparently supportive of everything. He had it in the back pocket of his blue jeans while he was hitchhiking. I don't know how he managed not to lose it.

Sultana and I stopped in Germany on the way to Sultana's sister's wedding, I believe it was 1966. That was the first time my wife met my family, although my parents had come to the wedding. She was very much appreciated, and she was very happy with all of it. Then we continued to go to East Pakistan for the wedding. Over there, the family met us at the airport. Most people spoke English because it had been a British colony. Because her father was well-respected in the area we got some preferential treatment moving through the lines at the airport. There were lots of interesting things for me to see and learn. For example, my wife told me I couldn't shake hands with her mother or touch her at all.

For my first dinner there, my mother-in-law cooked British food for me and Indian food for everyone else. I refused to eat the British food, though I appreciated that she had gone to the trouble. In fact, my brother had done the same thing. I think I was very much embraced in many ways by the family.

My father-in-law was Muslim but he drank occasionally, even though alcohol is prohibited for practicing Muslims. We had, at some point, brought something for him, but it was all locked up because of this rule. But he took me to a British club because he thought I would want beer. Even though I'm German, I'm not the beer-drinking kind but I appreciated his effort to embrace me, to do whatever he thought would please me. On the way, I asked—insisted actually—on going through the old city of Taka. That was a Hindu neighborhood; it was dark with narrow streets, little shops, and a Hindu temple. Muslims don't usually want to go there, but he had been there several times in his capacity as a doctor. He was reluctant to take me but did and was always with me to protect me.

There were lots of relatives around because of the wedding. They invited me to various places in their family. In some sense, I was almost the star. I didn't want to play that role, but it was very clear. The wedding itself was a huge Indian wedding. The women were in one room and the men were in another, but they could all see the ceremony. During the ceremony, the bride and groom could not see each other, but they were given a mirror to see each other for the first time, supposedly. It was an amazing event with lots of people, and I just enjoyed it.

We were there for a week. In some sense, I was prepared, through Sultana, for the cultural issues, and I was very excited. As a German, when I was a student, we hitchhiked a lot, but only in Europe, which was a totally different culture. I was curious about why certain things happened and I learned an enormous amount. I learned, particularly, to appreciate this very different culture.

I also enjoyed learning about their different kinds of habits. For example, a person came to the door to sharpen knives. There were so many merchants that went to sell things, and it was fascinating. And the family was also different. People came to the backyard and helped with cooking, but I was not supposed to go talk to them. Sultana's mother was very nice. She didn't speak English though she did learn a little. It was not that much, but it was enough to have a little bit of a conversation.

After the wedding it was soon time to go back to America. We had a stop in Delhi, in India. There I made a big mistake—I ate something from a street vendor. I reasoned I could do this because it was a mango and the seller peeled the mango with a knife; I thought that this knife had peeled many, many mangoes, and once peeled, it would be fine to eat. But I got sick. I was so sick that the next day I had to stop over in Karachi, in West Pakistan, and go to the hospital. It was pretty bad. That's when Sultana decided she wanted to go back and stay with her family longer. She thought our visit had been too short for her. I had to get back to Penn to teach, but she had friends who lived in Karachi, and this couple took care of me and brought me to the airport. So, I went back to the United States while she went back to spend more time with her parents.

By 1968, I believe, the sister and her new husband got divorced. Once the marriage ended, she felt she could never get married again in East Pakistan, so she came to the United States and stayed with us. We received her well. I managed to get her a fellowship to study at Temple University. She studied there, graduated, and later married someone from Penn, Ambrose Davis.

Sabbatical in Germany, 1970

In 1970, I got an invitation to teach in Berlin for their spring semester. I had a sabbatical that year and so we went. This was the first time Sultana really lived in Germany. The university rented a villa for us. The idea was that I would accept an offer to teach permanently there based on this shorter teaching experience.

Before it was time to go back to Philadelphia, we went on a quick trip to East Germany; I wanted to show Sultana Halberstadt and where I came from. We drove to Schwanebeck and I talked to the woman who was still there. I hadn't been since 1945. She remembered me of course.

Then we went to Halberstadt, where I looked up my old violin teacher, the one who had all the students learn together as a group. I thought I'd check to see if she was still alive. My wife came with me. She was, but had become badly disabled. She lived on the third or fourth floor of an apartment building. I rang the doorbell, and she came down with some difficulty. We had a good conversation. One of the things I found out was that when she was young, she had been in the Wandervogel.

We stayed at a hotel, which was also interesting. This was close to where we had lived, where we were bombed out, and it was the house of the Klumhold family. One of their sons had been executed by Hitler because he was involved in the July 20th effort to kill him. I knew the family; I knew this was next door to the hotel. We went there, and it turned out that the youngest daughter of this guy was actually a classmate of my sister, Ute. She went on to West Germany later and became the first television anchorwoman in West Germany. There were lots of these strange connections.

This trip was just to give Sultana a bit of a sense of Germany and what my life had been like. Parts of the trip were very good, but she also had some bad experiences. She went shopping in a grocery store and the cashier wouldn't wait on her. That made her really angry. She threw away all the apples she bought and said she'd never come back again. There were cultural differences that she noticed. When we went to East Germany, we went to a restaurant to eat. She was in a sari and I had a black beard. Now, a black beard—or beards in general—were not kosher in East Germany so we were a strange couple, and people stared at us. It was almost uncomfortable.

Academically it wasn't a good fit either because Germany was very underdeveloped as far as communications were concerned and there were many problems with student demonstrations. All of these were reasons against staying in Germany. When Sultana first came to the United States, she went through Germany and had been hosted for a short time by a German family in Frankfurt. She had the best of experiences in Frankfurt, so she was prejudiced positively. Overall, it was okay with me if she didn't want to live in Germany because I was also not quite so happy to go there, but because of academic reasons.

Sultana got pregnant in 1970 and we went back to Philadelphia. For her dissertation, it was beneficial for her to go to the British Library and the Royal Library. She was writing about the British understanding of the population in India. She had some interesting findings. Mainly, the British asked the population all kinds of questions, like "What is your religion?" and people didn't care; they were very religious by Western standards, but all had different religions. You went to your local church or local holy place, but it didn't really matter. There were many gods, not just one. So, the British found that when they asked what someone's religion was, they might respond by saying they were a blacksmith because it didn't really mean anything to them.

Sultana was looking at this and found an interesting thesis: when people don't even know what religion this is and then we suddenly impose this category, they become aware of each other. They become aware that the neighboring village is Muslim not Hindu. And in fact, maybe that created some of the divisions.

In London, Sultana stayed with my brother-in-law, Thomas Slater, the brother of Eve, my brother Ekkehart's wife. First, she stayed with them for a while, then took a separate apartment with another East Pakistani. We corresponded constantly.

In the meantime, the person who was now the dean at Urbana came to me and said her time was up. They couldn't let her be a candidate anymore; she had to submit her dissertation. I asked them to let her be, so they did. She came back from England and continued writing.

Around Christmas in 1970, my parents visited. Sultana finished the dissertation four days before Kaihan was born. I think her motivation was that she wanted to finish the dissertation before a different life with a child would start.

Section 4: Marriage and Children

The Birth of Kaihan

For the birth on February 19, Sultana was at a hospital downtown, which is now part of the University of Pennsylvania hospitals. On the day before, we went to IHOP and we went shopping. There was a soup she wanted to make, and we bought ingredients for that. My brother visited during the birth. We spent time in the hospital while she was in labor. I was in the waiting room during the birth, but I was almost immediately in the delivery room when the baby arrived. When they showed me the baby he was crying, unlike my daughter, who did not cry. We chose the name Kaihan—a Farsi name—very carefully because it had to be pronounced easily in the west. Kaihan made a lot of sense.

After the birth, I got an alarmist call from Sultana while she was still in the hospital that she could not breastfeed. It's not always automatic; one has to be a little patient. But she was totally upset. The nurses solved it somehow. Then, I picked them up and brought them to our house on Osage Avenue in West Philadelphia, where we'd bought a two-level house. When we drove home, the mileage of my car when we parked said 7,777.7, and I thought this was a good sign. My son would be a mathematician or very important person, which is why we gave him the middle name "Pascal." And Kaihan is an important person.

It was fun to have a baby. I was the one who changed the diapers all the time. Sultana couldn't do it. At that time, we didn't have Pampers. He was an easy baby. We had a garden in the back, and he played there.

Klaus holding Kaihan

There were three families who were close friends: One was a United Church minister who came from somewhere else and had no family, and who lived close to us on 46th Street. His name was Ralph Moore, and his wife was Jane. Another was a Philadelphia artist with whom I shared an office, Sam Maitin, whose wife, Lilyan, was also a friend. We three families had Thanksgiving together several times and we've kept this tradition alive for fifty years; the parents are dead, but the children are still doing it.

Sultana always said we all needed to have some sort of a vacation place for summers. In 1970, Sam, Ralph the minister, and I took a trip to Bucks County and other places, but we couldn't find anything. We found one place we wanted to buy, but the person who wanted to sell it to us asked for our names and then said something about a Jew boy (Sam and Lilyan were Jewish). That killed any possibility of going to this area. But in 1971, after Kaihan's birth, we found a place in the town of Sunbury in Northumberland County, and we bought it.

There was nothing there except a springhouse. We were told that it would be available to us and we could build something, but it turned out not to be part of the land; it was feeding a neighboring house. This is fifty-eight acres, a big place, and we still have it. The three families are landowners. We went there in '71 with my mother when Kaihan was very young. There was nothing on the land, and we camped with tents. Later on, I wanted to build three geodesic domes close together and have a little village there, but we couldn't really agree to that. I ended up building one with everyone else and they call it the Klaus house.

Friends of East Bengal

In March of 1971, the West Pakistan army went to East Pakistan to squash their movement of independence. It was a military intervention and it was pretty bad. We had very little knowledge in the West of what exactly happened except the news telling us that the West Pakistani military was there. Sultana gathered lots of friends from East Pakistan to discuss what they should do. There was one engineer who suggested collecting money for machine guns. He said he could bomb Pakistani ships, and he knew how to build a bomb. Now, this was crazy and we weren't interested in that. Then a group of Quakers joined us and got us thinking about what could be most harmful for the West Pakistanis politically.

Section 4: Marriage and Children

The Quakers focused on the fact that West Pakistan had gotten a lot of weapons from the United States, with ships coming to the harbors in Philadelphia and Baltimore to pick up these weapons. They suggested we could protest that. So, we built an organization. My suggestion was not to use the word Bangladesh in its name, even though that's the name they wanted to call it, but Friends of East Bengal instead. We formed a whole network of former East Pakistanis and friends, plus the Quakers. We launched an amazing movement of protests in Philadelphia. There is a book and a documentary movie, both called *Blockade,* about this. It was shortly after the Vietnam War so the police were very tricky, but the Quakers taught me that it was possible to get the police on our side. What the Quakers did—and what I learned later on to do—was ask them to join us. We told the police we were making a peaceful demonstration; they could see us. They came and protected us.

We went to the Harbor to protest and marched through Philadelphia with a flag. Much of it was publicized and Sultana was a little worried it would be too visible. We knew that West Pakistan targeted intellectuals...and by intellectuals, I mean that in East Pakistan the literacy rate was something like 10%, so her father stood out easily. (Indeed, we found out later on that her family had gone into hiding.) We didn't have any clue what was going on, but we were very good organizers. I was at the Annenberg School and I had the great advantage of a Xerox machine. I was the one who made the newsletter and copied *The New York Times* articles, which we distributed to cars driving by.

To stop a ship is not easy. Some demonstrators decided to use kayaks to throw themselves against the ship. That is not only dangerous, it's useless. These were big boats with a front that was two stories high. A kayak means nothing in comparison. One of the things that was particularly outstanding was that we mobilized so many people. A student of mine, who unfortunately died recently, went there with a kayak and was arrested by the Philadelphia Harbor police. They thought us unsafe, and rightly so. But the officer who pulled his kayak over said, "Look, if I had no uniform, I would be on your side."

We really had the population on our side. We also demonstrated in Baltimore, where many more ships came through. And we went to Congress. There was a lobbying group that was against giving any military aid to West Pakistan. I went and talked to some senators. It was an amazing movement and lasted almost until the end of 1971.

Later on, in December 1971, the Indian army went in and basically threw the West Pakistanis out. Luckily they didn't annex anything—

they left. This was the beginning of East Pakistan's independence movement. We decided we had to go to Bangladesh. Shortly before Christmas, we booked the flight. Kaihan was not even a year old, and between Philadelphia and Frankfurt, he cried the whole time. I convinced two of our traveling companions to let us go to Frankfurt, with the thought that we'd go to my parents. We left the plane, saying we'd take the next flight, and then I rented a car to get to my parents' house. My parents had never seen the baby and now we were standing in front of them, holding the baby, and they had no idea we were coming. Ekkehart and Eve were also there for Christmas. We spent two or three days there and then we went on, taking Kaihan with us.

We went to Kolkata next, but we couldn't get a flight from Kolkata to Dhaka (where Sultana's family is from) because there were only military flights, not private flights. We went through all kinds of channels trying to get a flight so that Sultana's family could meet the baby. That was a big event for us. It brought us very close together. It also brought us closer with other families and I'm still in touch with some Bengali people. This was when we found out her family had gone into hiding. We knew that they were liberated and had already indirectly heard that they were alive and fine. Her mother was clever enough to have placed a West Pakistani flag in front of her house, and she said that is what saved them.

The 1970s

When we returned from this trip, we realized we should get a bigger house so I started looking around. We bought a new house on Osage, several houses down. It was almost abandoned but had three levels. Then Sultana got pregnant with Heike. I had hoped that Heike would be born in the new house, but it was a very slow process to get the financing. So, she was born in the old house, and then we moved and that was a great thing.

That new house was published in *The Philadelphia Inquirer* as an outstanding renovation. It had been abandoned at some point and we completely renovated it. There were several apartments and a staircase going immediately up to the second floor, and the third floor was an apartment. When we bought it, the copper pipes in the basement had been stolen. It was really pretty bad, but the renovations were very innovative.

Section 4: Marriage and Children

Maybe because of the connection with the Quakers, my wife got a good job at St. Christopher's Hospital. This was a project financed by the U.S. government to find ways to get immigrants who had strange conceptions about medical practices to come to the hospital. There was a population around that area that wouldn't trust doctors. Sultana was writing books with one of the Quakers. She was fully employed there and was actually pretty effective. When she got pregnant with Heike, I don't know for sure, but I think she got very restless. In 1974, two weeks after Heike was born in July, Sultana wanted to have a babysitter so she could get back to work. She got a teaching job at St. Joseph Hospital and later on at Drexel.

The last time I went to Bangladesh was 1975, and as usual we went via Germany to spend some time there for Christmas. But then something very strange happened in Bangladesh. My wife fought constantly with her father. I thought that was unusual. She also fought with me at some point. Her father later approached me, saying, "Klaus, I know you have difficulties in marriage, but believe me, I had difficulties too." I didn't think that I had great difficulties. There's always tension somewhere. I was shocked that he mentioned that and mentioned himself as having had difficulties in his marriage. She was fighting for nothing, from my point of view. That was weird to me.

Though I never returned to Bangladesh, Sultana and I were connected to her side of the family. We brought Samina over from Bangladesh to stay with us and got her into Agnes Irwin School for Girls in Bryn Mawr. I stayed close to Samina and her husband, Will Reese, and to Najma and Ambrose Davis, as well as the children of these couples.

A few years later, I had a guest professorship in Holland for a spring. We were living in the Hague in the southern suburbs, near the border. We constantly went to the beach. It was very nice. That year, we spent Christmas in Germany, and Sultana continued on to Bangladesh.

Kaihan had to speak and write in Dutch there. He wrote an essay entitled "Mijn Vader," or "My Father." I cannot read it, but I must have it somewhere. I remember when I brought him to school for the first time that he was scared stiff. The teacher said that they knew English well but because this was a Dutch school, they would not speak English and he would have to learn, which he did.

Heike was only five and we took her to kindergarten there; it was right in front of our house. At some point, I asked her how she liked it and who she played with. She said, "I don't care. If people want to play with me, they can." The other kindergarten parents liked having children around who spoke other languages and were pleased Heike was there. One day I heard Kaihan and Heike arguing about something in our house. I didn't know what it was about and when I stopped to listen I realized they were arguing with each other in Dutch.

Meanwhile, Sultana and I struggled as a couple and eventually the marriage ended. After living with and loving each other for years, studying for the same academic degree with so much to learn, bringing up two children anyone would be proud of, sharing exciting experiences traveling the world, fighting together for the right things with remarkable success, and maintaining warm family relationships across continents, I still cherish what Sultana and I accomplished together and the memories I share with many family members and friends.

My Children

Following the divorce, I stayed in Philadelphia while Sultana pursued jobs in various places. The child custody agreement was complicated but I made it work, and am close to both Kaihan and Heike.

In 1989, Kaihan started at Penn. He graduated with a BA in 1994. He actually started in the school of engineering but then shifted to Wharton, and after that, he got an MBA from Columbia University. There, he found something very interesting: a Chinese book called *Thirty-Six Stratagems*. It's one of those Chinese how-to-run-an-army books. He thought that would be good to translate into business terms in America and wrote a book on that. He got a job at McKinsey but stayed only for four years, then got a PhD in Finland. He is now an amazing consultant for big businesses and is invited to give workshops on topics like innovation. His clients are Boeing, Coca-Cola, and Starbucks. He is traveling the world right now. When you Google him, he has written more books than I have. He's an amazing inspirational speaker—TED Talk-like things.

Kaihan married Pilar Ramos, who attended Penn with him and then graduated from the University of Pennsylvania Law School. We spent many happy days with Pilar and her parents both in Philadelphia and in New Orleans, and in the various places they lived (i.e., South Beach and Greenwich). I was always happy to attend events at my grandchildren's school in Greenwich.

Heike went to a boarding school at Loomis Chaffee School in Connecticut around the time Kaihan went to Penn. She came to study at Penn three years later and started playing soccer there, serving as captain during her two final years at Penn. (She had played at Loomis Chaffee and had been captain of her team.) She met her husband, Brendan Sullivan, there; they're both soccer players. They have four children and all of them play soccer, with one playing professional soccer with the Philadelphia Union. After Penn, she went to law school. We always spent Christmas Eve with Heike, her family, and her husband's family. It was always the highlight of the year, with my daughter cooking an amazing meal. Once she even attempted to make a Dresden Stollen, which was a great treat for me.

To me, it's amazing. When you have children, you see them always as children. Recently, we were struggling with my will. I know that this is her specialty (she is the head of the trusts and estates group at her law firm, Ballard Spahr, where she is a partner), so we asked her to be part of the Zoom talk with the lawyer. It's amazing what she knew. I was totally flabbergasted. She is an amazing person.

I maintained a relationship with Germany with my children. I'm happy to say I made sure that my children were connected with their cousins. That was my main mission, that they not lose contact. I took them to Austria to go skiing. Later on, they went by themselves. In addition, we had several family reunions, including one in Halberstadt shortly after my father died in 2002. He was almost 102. We went to Berlin, in a sort of eco-village and we had a reunion in Cape May, New Jersey, in a huge house by the beach. The last family reunion was in 2017, on a huge farm-like compound in the Netherlands that had tents, houses, apartments, swimming, soccer fields, and many other activities. Each Krippendorff family was represented, as well as Marge's grandson Owen. The many children played soccer for hours, and stayed up all night playing board games and laughing. One of my grandchildren—I believe it was Lucas—built a huge tower of slats or blocks that must have been ten feet tall.

Sultana's and Klaus's wedding

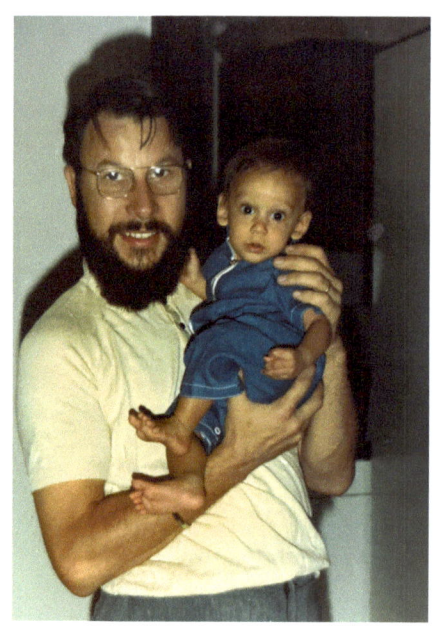

Klaus with his children

Section 4: Marriage and Children

Sultana, Klaus holding newborn Heike, and Kaihan

Klaus: A Memoir

The Krippendorff family in West Philadelphia

Section 4: Marriage and Children

*Kaihan, Sultana, Herbert, and Klaus
with Heike on his shoulders*

A Krippendorff Christmas

Section 5
Career

Annenberg and Communications

The term "communication" is old, but as a discipline it is relatively new. In the United States, at Iowa, they wanted to change the journalism department into one of communication, realizing there were many more ways of communication than newspapers, like radio and television. Then came information theory with mathematics that had to do with cryptography, trying to find out enemy communications.

With the arrival of mathematics, communication suddenly became a discipline in academia. In addition to content analysis, I taught a basic course, Models of Communication. Later on came two advanced courses: One was Message Analysis, which went along with content analysis, looking at the flow of messages in networks. The other was around cybernetics and society. Those were my main graduate courses. I also taught an undergraduate course on cybernetics and communication.

We called it a pro seminar. That means that the first-year students had to take one course that was organized by the dean, George Gerbner. He invited people from the faculty to give presentations and I was one of them. There were lots of topics presented that I did not quite agree with. For example, function. The dean was saying something about the function of communication. So, I presented something like forty different meanings of function. One doesn't need to think of one only. For many students, the pro seminar was not such a good experience because Gerbner had the idea that after each lecture everyone had to write at least half a page about what they got out of it, so there was good feedback for the teacher. I thought that was a good idea. But he graded them on it, and most of them were Ds. His philosophy was that if you give a bad grade it will motivate the student to excel, which of course is ridiculous. In fact, it created just the opposite. The students thought, *Why are we here?* At that time, there were lots of student revolutions in Annenberg against the pro seminar and the teaching and so on.

This was in the '60s. Fifty years later, we had the first and only reunion of students graduating that I overlapped with, graduating a year after I had been there. It was a whole weekend of classes and lectures, followed by a lovely dinner held at the Union League of Philadelphia. Those students knew me well. I had been a student as well, and I connected with them. Annenberg was an amazing place. There was a television studio; I'd never been in one. I went there, observed, and chatted with them. I was the only one who they knew, and they celebrated me. I said, "Don't celebrate me. Celebrate yourself. Tell your stories." I heard amazing stories about that time. It was really miserable for many of them.

Krippendorff's Alpha

The Violence Project was early in my career. It was very formative for me. One post-doctoral fellow, who was Black, had studied prejudices against Black people on television. He noticed that most roles on television for Black people were inferior roles: they were made fun of, they were the villain. There was also a visitor from Holland who knew a lot about public opinion and statistics. At some point George Gerbner was asked by the Surgeon General to create data of violence on television in the United States. There was a movement in the Senate to talk about the influence of television violence on people. They were concerned that violence was not very healthy and wondered what one could do about it. Gerbner called the three of us in to discuss the project. It was of national importance and couldn't be treated in a small way. It had to be respectable.

We decided to help. There was a very short time limit. We taped a lot of television shows and started developing coding instruments to capture who the villain was, what was being done to different characters, what were the qualities of the police, etc. It turned out that this coding was unreliable—people saw things differently. If everyone disagreed on what they were seeing, the findings could not be reliable. The coders, who were largely students, generally had other interests but wanted to get money or experience. These were all things that made it difficult to find reliable data. People from television studios would say it was not useful, and psychologists would say that violence on television was a way of diverting real violence to make it symbolic. There were also many parties against the study, so we had to be confident in our findings.

I thought about other ways we could do this study. At that point I was an expert in information theory, and I used it to measure the degree to which two or more coders agreed. It turned out that information theory had certain biases, which would not be applicable. I couldn't do that. I had to shift it. Then I found another kind of method: variance analysis. One could do this more easily, but it was not applicable to our more categorical descriptions of the victims and so on. It was applicable only to when you had a scale with numbers and not with categories, and ours were mostly categories. I had to extend that theory.

At Christmas I was on a plane to East Pakistan and had nothing else to do on the long flight, so I worked and worked. Then I found the clue: when one looked at variance analysis slightly differently, one could change it to a categorical type. That's when I developed a coefficient alpha for agreement, to make that possible. This coefficient was very elaborate to compute. We had a table with several people and we distributed the task. The first one had to count categories, the second one had to multiply, things like that. We got some results, but the process was just terrible. I decided I had to learn computer programming, so I went to the electrical engineering department. They had a course on what was then Fortran IV, the latest computer language. I learned to program and wrote the program for that coefficient. We could take the data that the students provided, put it on Hollerith cards (punch cards), and take them to the computer center, and they would compute it with my program and give us the data the next day. Even with these innovations, it was still very limiting.

I kept working at developing the coefficient. At that time, I really didn't know the literature, but other people did. There were some other coefficients that were proposed, like Scott's Pi, which was created by an opinion researcher. This was very similar to mine but limited to two people's data, and we had more than two coders. In psychology, there's a coefficient called the X-ray Reliability Coefficient, but it was really more psychological—whether there would be an underlying theory in the way people respond to tests. Even though I didn't know the literature much, I realized that my coefficient was much better than what already existed. I published a few things about this, and other people got interested. I got in touch with many researchers who had similar problems and tried to solve them. I learned what other people's problems were, not just mine.

It turned out that our violence data was never challenged. There were people who wrote against the idea that violence was bad, but not that our findings were bad. But there were misunderstandings. George Gerbner's position was that calculating reliability was meaningless because the industry was interested in creating something that was so ambiguous that you couldn't hold them responsible. That meant they really wanted the analysis to be unreliable. If that was true, to me it just meant that we had to find out where the ambiguity came from and make sure that was be reliable, too.

My alpha took off and I wrote many articles on it. Recently, I've been working on a book called *The Reliability of Generating Data*. It covers lots of areas: how ambiguous many dictionary entries are, among others. This is mainly what I'm known for, but I find it is only a side thing. I feel bad that this is considered one of my major academic contributions; I don't think it is.

Armor and Cultural Context

I went once with my children to the Philadelphia Museum of Art, where there is a collection of arms and armor. The collection includes some black armor from the Count of Brunswick. I knew from the history of mythology that supposedly there was in Germany a black knight who came at night and corrected injustices. I told my children the story of the black knight. Later on, I found out that he was in Brunswick and had the armor made in his backyard. I wrote a paper about the shifting of cultural objects. What was the meaning of this armor when the people were making it? If the client came and said it didn't fit or he didn't like it, it had to be changed. That made it a totally different object for the maker. At the same time, when used in war, where people were fearful of being hurt when jumping off their horse or fighting on foot with a sword, it had a different meaning. And in Germany, after the knights became less important, then came the collectors—how much money is this worth, what is the history of it, how should I present it? At the Art Museum, the armors are from a single collector who bought all of them when traveling through Europe. When he died he gave all of it to the Art Museum. On display is a photo of his living room full of armor, before he gave it away. There's another meaning there. Everything has a different meaning. I made a long theory about how the meaning of objects systematically changes in the cultural context.

Design/Product Semantics

When I came to the United States, I was basically sidetracked. I did not do anything design related, though I stayed in contact with many of my design friends from Ulm. One of them, Reinhart Butter, was two years younger than me; we were good friends, and he later became a professor at Ohio State University (OSU). He was in the design department, and he purchased my thesis and always carried it with him. He invited me to give two lectures and a workshop, so I went to OSU several times, and in 1984 he came to me and said, "I have a sabbatical and I want to do something with the ideas you developed in your thesis. We have to write something together."

He came to Philadelphia to visit me and we started writing a paper. We didn't finish it; when someone sits next to me and talks, I cannot write, only outline things. Later in 1984, we both edited a journal article for the Industrial Designers Society of America (*Innovation* magazine). There we proposed the idea of product semantics, the idea of looking at the meaning of objects. My axiom was that people didn't react to the physical qualities of objects, but reacted to what the physical qualities meant to them. Yes, physicality was there, but it meant nothing if it didn't mean something to the person looking at it.

Our approach spread like a fire through the design community and generated many meetings and workshops. That same year, the Association for Industrial Designers organized a summer workshop over ten days. It was held at a famous art university in Detroit. There were thirty or forty people. We had a very successful one-week workshop, making or proposing something under the guidance of always looking at the meaning of objects.

In 1985, Philips (located in Eindhoven, Netherlands) approached me. They made electronics, which appealed to me. They were changing their philosophy in the design department and asked me and designers all over the world to come and give input. Three of us went. We tried to shift their perception toward the issue of meaning and were very successful. One of the products that later became important was a radio that you could carry around, like a boom box. The interesting thing, which I always cite in other contexts, was that when the head of the design department took the design developed in this workshop to the marketing people and told them he wanted to produce it, he got a lot of pushback. The marketers did a study and said it couldn't be produced—it was too far-out and outlandish. But the department head had a friend in Italy who saw it and wanted a thousand of them. So, he pushed his new design, and it ended up being a major success.

At that time, I was at Annenberg. In a sense, all of this design work was unconnected to Annenberg, except philosophically. There was a design conference in Holland, where I gave a presentation. Someone from Helsinki invited me and some others to organize a weeklong workshop on product semantics. The workshop results were published, and then they held two more conferences every year. It really took off. Reinhart Butter and I were invited to so many places. In Japan, I gave a workshop at the invitation of a former Ulm student, who was Japanese and had become chair of a design school. I went to Germany, too. The Germans were far behind other countries in this way of thinking. In Dublin, I got an award for the best article published in *Design Management Journal*. I was invited several times to teach at Kalmar in Sweden, in the design department. They later gave me a doctor of philosophy.

Not long after that, I took a sabbatical and Reinhart Butter invited me to spend a semester at OSU. I was appointed "advanced professor in design in systems engineering." The University of the Arts here in Philadelphia invited me to give two courses during my sabbatical. In the meantime, I wrote many small papers. I had an office in the design department of OSU, but mainly worked in a consulting firm. The head of an experimental design laboratory wanted me to be there. Now, I was an odd person. I was a designer, but I was not really known for design. In the beginning, they gave me an office, but didn't really know how to use me. Then at some point someone asked if I had any ideas about designing a washing machine. I did have some ideas, and they liked them a lot. From that moment on, I was on every design team.

A totally different department at Philips in Eindhoven heard about product semantics and contacted this advanced experimental design laboratory to see if they could send someone to observe how they work. It was very unsystematic, how we worked, and they thought that there was a method to learn and import from us. We went from Ohio to Holland several times. They wanted to develop a system for insurance companies to handle insurance claims, which was the social part. But they wanted to make computers that would do that. Included in the discussion, then, were people who worked in computers, computer programmers, management, marketing. We had to present certain ideas to them. It was, in my opinion, very primitively cooked up. But it changed their way of thinking.

In Ohio, they did some minor studies taking videos of people working on insurance claims. The idea was to incorporate that into a future design. For about half a year, I went back and forth to Holland, even after I had returned to Annenberg. It was torturous. But it was a very practical exercise. It derived out of this movement toward what is now called "human-centered" design. The idea of meaning is still very important to me.

I was asked to be the chair of the department at USC in Berkeley, which is where my former thesis advisor was teaching. I think he was the one to put my name out there. I went there and gave lectures I'd prepared very carefully, but I was not happy. I already had my feet in Annenberg, so I didn't really try to make it happen. But when they selected someone else I was disappointed. They didn't want to be challenged. I was also offered a deanship at Syracuse.

In 2009, I decided to put together the papers I'd written during my sabbatical in a book called *The Semantic Turn: A New Foundation for Design*. It was translated into Japanese, Hungarian, and German. It was my first book on design issues. I said that we had to think of design as changing, from product design or functional design to issues of branding, selling, meaning, organizing designers, language, designers' language, the discourse of design. I developed a trajectory of design which, I argued, we had to march to. That is quoted frequently.

I don't think the idea itself was so revolutionary because people have always had to think about selling a product when they were designing it. That element was always there. My complaint was that designers were limited to marketing esthetics. Usually at some point, an object needs to be practical. It needs to exist and work in real life. The idea of function did not go very far technologically. I said that we had to extend the idea of a producer to not just marketing. That's what they had always hired designers to do, to improve marketability, but nothing else was of interest because it didn't generate revenue. My point was that one had to think of the long-range implications of each element.

I traveled all over the world to design conferences. There was a big conference in India and I was the key presenter. It was fascinating because they had certain ideas about design already, but I provided them with a conceptual framework. India has a different culture and they felt that Western ideas were often imposed upon them. I was always saying that we had to respond to them and *contribute* to their culture, not just to the profit of the manufacturer.

I went to Bogota, Columbia, several times to give lectures. They were so enthused that they held a one-week workshop, and it was amazing. I was invited to Turkey to give some lectures in Ankara. There was a bigger design department in Constantinople (Istanbul), which invited me over when they heard I was in Ankara. I'd wanted to go to Constantinople because there is more interesting architectural history there. They treated me very well.

At some point there was a conference in Basel, and there was a competing philosophy by someone who founded another area. He called it product language. I would say that products don't speak language, humans do. It's our own thing to impose. I didn't give a lecture there, but I met a young Turkish woman, a designer who had presented something. Turkish people have a whole culture of tea glasses and rituals, so she made a study of tea drinking. I made some suggestions on how to approach that. Later on, while working toward a PhD in Turkey, she reached out to me to say she was coming to Philadelphia and asked for my help. I managed to get her an office at Annenberg for a year. Initially, she wanted to write her dissertation on ironing boards. I said, "Who uses ironing boards nowadays?" In Turkey, lots of people do, but there's not that much in it. She then changed the topic and was thinking of how people perceive health issues. She came here and linked up with health communities on the internet, like *Weight Watchers*. She became part of this community mainly to find out what could be done about their concerns. She taped everything and wanted to give this to designers to see what they could do with it. A former student of Reinhart Butter's was teaching design at Drexel, and I recruited her to help this Turkish student condense her learnings—highlight key things in a few pages. We invented a technique, which was amazing (inspired by my work in content analysis). We gave them three pens: yellow, red, and green. They had to underline things that were unusual, that they learned something from, and that gave an idea of a product. When these designers—who had never really done any ethnographic research—said, "Oh my God, I never thought about it through these kind of lenses," I felt I had really accomplished something important.

She wrote her dissertation in Turkey, and I flew over for the dissertation defense. I was the principal advisor; although as a foreigner I was not really in charge of the committee, it was really exciting to see what she did.

I did all this in parallel to my job at Annenberg. It was a lot of time spent developing ideas that had nothing to do with communication.

Cybernetics

When I was in Oxford, England, while still a student at Ulm, I'd bought a book by Ross Ashby, *Introduction to Cybernetics,* which had been published just three or four years before. Later, it turned out to be the key book on cybernetics, kind of an introduction with his special twist, but Norbert Wiener was actually the inventor of the name cybernetics, in part. There were even earlier users. Ampère defined it as a theory of government. The word *cybernetics* comes from Greek, referring to the steersmen of a boat. The boat is influenced by many things, like wind, but the sailor has to control it. That was Ampère's idea, using that for the science of government. Wiener used it for control for a circle or feedback mechanisms. He was a mathematician and his book was called *Cybernetics or Control and Communication in The Animal and The Machine.* It had to do with communication and control. But Ashby said that there were so many equations, very sophisticated ones, the idea would get lost unless you put it down in a more easy-to-understand way. This is what he did, and that's the reason why I think he became increasingly important in the cybernetic community.

From 1962 to 1963, I took a course from Ashby at Urbana. That was a very important influence, which gave me a way to structure my thinking that I had not thought about before, the idea of systems, feedback, of governing ideas—for example, one of Ashby's theories was that the biological organism is somewhat a self-governing system. All the organs do things that keep you alive. There was an idea that maybe that should be a focus of cybernetics because they're all connected to preserve the life of the organism. There were so-called self-organizing systems. Even organizations are, in some sense, self-organizing. The University of Pennsylvania makes rules about itself and isn't really copying someone else. Or maybe they do, but they make their own decisions. So much of the social world is also self-organizing.

Ashby was very mathematically oriented. He invented a different kind of scientific approach. Most scientists make observations or experiments, but he said we should have a different approach for cybernetics. We had an idea, then we made a model and tested whether it did what we wanted it to do. It would be a science of the models and not the real world—that would be secondary. He said, correctly, that if you want to make an economic measure, you can't experiment with a whole country and then see that it doesn't work. You have to have a model to test it first. Ultimately, building models meant using computers, although at some point he had very mechanical types of models.

I went to the first conference of the American Society for Cybernetics in Gainesville, Maryland. I had an interesting experience, and only later on did I realize the importance of it. It involved the anthropologist Margaret Mead. Immediately after the war, from 1946 to 1953, the Macy's Foundation in New York funded a meeting of the most advanced scholars in the United States on cybernetics. During that time, the notion of cybernetics became formalized and defined. There were mainly engineers and cognitive scientists, but the anthropologists Margaret Mead and Gregory Bateson were there, too. It was a very interdisciplinary group.

Mead always saw the limitation of Wiener cybernetics, which was mathematical and mechanical, so most of the earlier cybernetics had to do with designing machines that automated things. There were lots of robots and mechanisms in production, all the result of the early cybernetic focus on mathematics. Mead gave the keynote there and said we had to change cybernetics. Cybernetics was not a science of feedback. Cybernetics was a science of solving problems in unusual ways. It was a language, she said, that was spoken by people, and cyberneticians had to take responsibility for what language does. That was totally unusual. She cited cases like automated defense mechanisms in the U.S. and Russia. She said this was very dangerous because we didn't really know the interaction. It was easily possible that a minor mistake could create major disasters. She said there were consequences when you communicated the idea of cybernetics in other fields and let them apply it. Later on, I took that idea as a very basic one to change the nature of cybernetics.

At the time of this conference I knew Ashby and Heinz von Foerster, but I didn't know many other cyberneticians. I was an assistant professor in communications then, so I was relatively low in the hierarchy, but I talked to people. After that conference, I went to almost every one of the conferences held by the Cybernetic Association. They were largely sponsored by the U.S. government because they saw that the Russians were doing the same thing, but better. At some point the financing stopped and the association declined a little. It ended up being a relatively small group in Washington, D.C., with no conferences or anything for a while. I decided, being at Annenberg, that we could hold a conference there. The administration was very uncertain, but they let me do it. They would get people to come to the conference, they would tape it, and I would organize it and edit the footage.

I gathered a group of people at the University of Pennsylvania to organize the conference with help from Fred Styer, Stu Applebaum, and others who were from other departments, decision sciences, electrical engineering, management, and other universities. We imitated the early cybernetics conference but on a smaller scale. In 1987, we had a very interesting conference. It was called Communication and Control in Society. There were amazing professors such as Anatol Rapoport and several others from the communication field. It was very exciting to see so many people coming together and doing things. But the cybernetics association didn't really support it much. They had not had a membership meeting for three years, and the guy who was in charge had been elected a long time ago and wasn't interested in reelection. It was basically a dying place.

The Philadelphia group, about ten of us, decided to have our own cybernetics meetings. I wrote a constitution and we talked with each other. The cybernetics association asked us to come back, and we said we would if they'd take our constitution and become a viable organization. They elected someone who I was close with as president. We talked and he managed to get our constitution introduced there. This was only a strategic element to make the cybernetic group viable and democratic. Since that happened there have been many meetings, and I have attended almost every one of them. In '84, we initiated the Gordon Conference on Cybernetics, in New England. We had two such conferences.

My push in the American Society for Cybernetics was to introduce the human element. This goes back to semantics. I wrote about the discourse of cybernetics. They have to be reflexive, meaning you have to know that you are part of it. I wrote many papers around this idea, and in all of them there was somehow the design spirit through memory. It's not enough to just describe something, you have to do something.

All this led to my receiving a Norbert Wiener Award from the American Society for Cybernetics, another from a European association, and then a medal for contribution to complexity signs. I received another award for making major contributions to cybernetics from Europe.

Right now, I'm working on a paper called "Critical Cybernetics." It discusses when cybernetics, particularly artificial intelligence, boxes people in to become almost like algorithms. When you have to go to city hall looking for an answer about something, you have to ask many questions to get what you need. You basically become a robot. You may be getting to an answer, but often not. That's a kind of an imposition of AI thinking to human activity. I have been giving several papers on the oppression of AI.

I'm also writing something more fundamental on the origin of social power, which many translate into physical things—you have power and you can force yourself onto others. Social power is taking place through language. So, one should not use physical metaphors to describe social relationships. I'm saying there are so many of what I call epistemological problems in language that we confuse domains like physics with human beings, and that creates problems. For example, there is an important system science in cybernetics when you talk about social organizations and how the social organization needs to be viable. What does viable mean? It means these functions have to be preserved. That is why I say it's a biological metaphor and it shouldn't be, because an organization is constituted by human beings. Human beings make a choice by saying they want to be part of this organization and take up certain types of roles. The organization is basically in the hands of those people. It's an abstraction that one can enact, not a reality. I'm shifting the idea of an organization from one that is self-organizing, viable, and everything else is subordinate to it, as much of sociology thinks of human beings as contributors to society or as being irrelevant or dysfunctional. I'm saying that we should turn it around and simply say that the organization should be the servant of the members.

As a result of my work with Ashby, I wrote a book on information theory that was published in '86. To my amazement, it is still being sold and is widely read. It is a small book, but it was critical. Cyberneticians always look at the circularities, but system sciences look at systems, parts, interactions. I went several times to meetings about system sciences. One was in Holland, where a famous computer scientist, George Klir, presented this idea. I saw all the parts that he described as interacting. None of them were circularly organized. As a cybernetician, that is where I thought we had to get into.

Then I found out that information theory is only about linear connections from here to there—information transmission—and fails to look at the circularity, what happens if there's feedback that changes it. Information theory incorporates the idea of circular phenomena. It turns out not to be possible to deal with probability theory, which is the basis of information theory. One has to have another way of thinking. I developed an algorithm to study this. This was one contribution to shift system sciences to look for more complex relationships.

The first course I taught at Annenberg was content analysis; we talked about data, but I also wanted to make a basic cause for communication. It's called Models of Communication. It's basically cybernetics and different ways one could look at that. And that led into another kind of seminar, Cybernetics in Society, how in social phenomena, the circle of feedback is present and incorporates the changes of one's own perceptions. That is my main contribution. I'm not always that successful because many cyberneticians don't understand my goal. But I'm always saying, "Language is important."

Conversation has to do with design. Ideas come through conversations. I would say that nowadays, conversations are evolutionary mechanisms that are faster than biological evolution. You can say something today and immediately get feedback—someone elaborates or ignores it, and there is an evolution going on. It's totally amazing. It's faster than any other evolution that human beings can engage in.

Other Important Publications

Very early on in the International Communication Association (ICA), my first paper was about introducing some cybernetic ideas in the area of communication. There was a communication theorist philosopher who said that communication was the study of who says what, to whom, with what effects, and they were different areas that one had to study separately. I thought it was bogus to say those are different disciplines because if you wanted to understand communication, you had to understand all these areas together. In 1971 I wrote a paper very much influenced by my cybernetic thinking of collecting data for communication research. My view was that we had to get data that linked the creator of communication with the audience, the content, everything. To me that just had to be studied as a dynamic system. It was my first ever paper and I submitted it to *The Journal of Communication,* which was then rather thin. The editor said that two reviewers wanted to reject it, but he, the editor, wanted it published and overrode the reviewers. It was given the first prize as the best article of the year.

Besides the book published in 1952 on content analysis that I'd criticized as being too limiting, there were no other books about this subject. I was approached by a publisher to write a book on content analysis, and it was published in 1980. It was translated into Farsi, Japanese, Spanish, Indonesian, and Hungarian. It is now in its fourth edition and is being translated into Chinese. I got an award from the International Communication Association for it being the most influential book in communication research.

(I should mention here that I was president of the ICA, though not at the time of these awards. When I first started, I thought we should have topics for each meeting, which was unheard of. One topic I chose was the future of communication because I saw so many changes one should look at. I had a committee to research who we could invite. Up to this point the meetings had been called conventions. I thought that wasn't academic and suggested we call it a conference. I wasn't a graphic designer, but I decided to design the conference brochure. I made lots of innovations. I was also credited as the first president who gave a paper on different ways of thinking of communication. That is much more common now.)

A publication that is not as successful as the content analysis book is the bulk pack I put together with a student of mine. The student and I co-authored this reader. It was composed of all the articles I asked students to read, and I am pleased with it even though it is not an actual book.

Memorable Students

I worked with incredible scholars and was very much supported by the deans of the Annenberg School. Those following George Gerbner as dean were prominent in their fields (Kathleen Hall Jamieson, Michael X. Delli Carpini, and John L. Jackson, Jr., the current Provost of the University). My Annenberg faculty members were critical to the work I did and were friends as well as colleagues, such as Barbie Zellzer, Joe Cappella, Oscar Gandy, Bob Hornik, Carolyn Marvin, Vincent Price (now president of Duke University), Joe Turow, to name but a few.

I had amazing students, and I worked with most of them very closely. I learned as much from them as they had learned from me. For example, Mary Brock, the one I co-edited the reader with, was a journalist and photographer. She wrote a dissertation on visual communication. I introduced a lot of interesting concepts that she's still drawing on. She developed the notion that visual communication was not enough by itself; you had to know what the image is. For example, that's why we have captions underneath pictures: because we cannot see unless we know the context.

Chuck Goodwin was one of my earliest students. He was hired as a student to be a videographer at the Child Guidance Clinic and wrote a dissertation about what was going on in conversations in all these videos he had. He developed a theory of conversation based on eye contact. If you lost eye contact, then you changed topics. If you didn't get eye contact, then you felt that you couldn't talk. Statements were always incomplete when eye contact was lost. He made many important observations. Some of my students were very insightful people.

James Taylor was Canadian and working in the television laboratory at the Annenberg School, trying to get a PhD. Over the summer he got a project for the Philadelphia Museum of Art, seeing what the museum could do to improve its visitor experience. He started seeing what was going on in the organization. He was increasingly interested in organization theory and communication in organizations, and he wrote a dissertation on that. Later on, he became the chair of the communications department in Montreal and had great students whom I got to know.

Nicole Keating was a documentary filmmaker. She interviewed people who made documentary films and developed a theory of how documentary films are made. It was about what I call the stakeholders of the film. They have all different perspectives: the one who shows it wants to make money; the historian wants to be sure it is historically accurate. She found that the people that are most disappointed are always the academics because they say it is not historically accurate, which conflicts with the filmmaker who wants to make something that has a narrative that's understandable.

Many of my graduate students have become professors at outstanding universities, such as Mariaelena Bartesaghi, an Italian student who received her PhD from Annenberg and is now a professor in St. Petersburg, Florida at the University of South Florida. Mariaelena, like many of my students, wrote an outstanding dissertation on therapeutic discourse titled "Disability in Dialogue" which won many awards.

Over the years, I worked with many students and learned as much from them as they learned from me, and many, I am happy to say, stay in touch with me.

Section 5: Career

International Posts

In 1970, I was invited to Berlin to teach a semester on communication at the Free University of Berlin's journalism department. But Germany was, at that time, very underdeveloped as far as communication was concerned. The journalism department was a big jump for me. It was difficult teaching at this school of journalism. Communication was not really accepted as an independent discipline. I taught whatever I wanted, and content analysis, which I knew a lot about. You could say I was a bit of a pioneer because I wanted to have a computer program for students' findings. I went to the computer center, and nobody from the social sciences had ever been there. I wrote a program there, and it worked.

In 1968, there had been a big student revolution all over Europe. It was very Marxist, very anti-establishment and against the dogmatism of some academics. I was in a classroom teaching content analysis when four or five people entered in the middle of the class and sat in the front row. This was not so unusual, but after a while they interrupted and said, "You're teaching capitalist methodology." I said it wasn't capitalist. They said, "Well, you are teaching American capitalist technology." I simply replied, "No. Why couldn't you use a computer to compute a revolution?" Many people don't want change no matter what political side they are on. There was still a great deal of unrest as far as student satisfaction was concerned. It was really tense. I realized that I would have to fight too much to be there, both with students and with the school administration, so I decided not to take the permanent teaching job.

During this time in Berlin, I was also invited by a famous scholar, Jürgen Habermas in the Frankfurt School, to give a lecture in his seminar. Afterward, he criticized me badly. He was right that I was focusing on something that I shouldn't. But I stayed in good connection with him. There were other openings in Germany accepting me as a scholar and I met other people in Frankfurt, but it was very different. People would call me Professor Krippendorff. I'm not accustomed to that. I'm Klaus. I met a man who said he was an assistant and was basically carrying this other professor's suitcase, seeing that the chalk was there for the blackboard. He did it for four years. I asked when he would be done and he didn't know. The whole hierarchy and the limited flexibility to newness didn't appeal to me. I had been in Ulm at this avant-garde school. Berlin was far from avant-garde. It wasn't for me.

In 1979 or 1980, I became a fellow for one year at the Netherlands Institute for Advanced Studies. You'd go there, do your thing, and participate in discussions with others. Half of them were from the Netherlands, and others were from various countries. I went to several conferences in Vienna and several places in Europe. When coming back from that, I was invited to Bremen in Germany, where I developed this combination of cybernetics and communication.

Most social scientists document what they find, describing facts and theories about it. There are endless theories about, for example, oppression, discrimination. To me, this was meaningless. I thought you had to find out what to do about it. One way to at least start understanding is to understand how what you describe as facts are actually created. Part of public opinion is created by things like newspaper articles and people want to exploit information for political purposes. One has to understand that social reality does not exist without someone having created it—even if unintentionally. Language plays a big role. I wrote a paper on the social construction of public opinion in Bremen, which was widely published and discussed. My approach is really about asking, how does it come about? Not what is.

Conclusion

Klaus passed away on October 10, 2022, before he could finish this book. To complete the telling of his life story, his children and wife shared memories of his later years, which were defined by his second marriage and time with his family, including grandchildren.

Meeting Marge and Family Weddings

In the twelve years after his separation from Sultana, Klaus dated a few women, including two old friends from Germany. Nothing stuck. When Klaus and Marge met, they were both coming out of divorces. Their lives were complicated at the time, but Marge felt from the very beginning that they had a special connection.

Their first date was on Memorial Day in 1994, at a coffee shop near the Philadelphia Museum of Art. When heading out of the coffee shop, they bumped into Kaihan, who was on his way to the museum—a notable coincidence since Kaihan went there very rarely. Klaus left soon after on a planned trip to Australia and Marge didn't know whether or not she would hear from him after that. But Marge remembers telling herself that if she didn't hear from him, she'd contact him, an approach she usually didn't take in her dating life. This ended up being a moot point; she received a postcard from Klaus in the middle of his trip. "As soon as I got that postcard, I knew we were on," she remembers.

Things moved fairly quickly from there. They spent lots of time at each other's houses, though Klaus didn't like Marge's kitchen. The second or third time he visited he brought a satchel of his tools with the aim of taking down a huge cupboard in the kitchen. It was an old house, and soon they were both sick from all the fumes and debris released as he worked. But he pulled the cabinet off and was soon meticulously measuring every square inch of the kitchen, making plans for a full renovation.

In 1996, Marge and Klaus bought a house together on 24th Street in Philadelphia. The next big event was Heike and Brendan's wedding—though that was a surprise. Heike called Klaus from a pay phone while on a break at her waitressing job at Circa. "Is Marge with you?" she asked. "Are you sitting down?" Then she shared her good news: she and Brendan had gotten married in Las Vegas. Klaus was surprised but immediately happy for the couple. He treated Brendan as part of the family—just as if he were one of Klaus's own children, he could do no wrong.

Marge and Klaus were the next to marry, on May 8, 1998, soon followed by Kaihan and Pilar's wedding in New Orleans. Kaihan had been concerned about his mother's and father's sides of the family coming together for a big wedding and getting photos with both his mom and dad together. But everyone was of the mind that it was important to come together for the big day. Sultana made sure to take photos with Klaus and Marge, and thanked Marge for being so nice to her children. To Klaus she said, "We did a good job with these kids." That was important to him.

With Kaihan, Pilar, Heike, Brendan, Marge, and cousin Kaya all having gone to Penn, lots of people at the wedding were from the school. At some point, the guests broke into "The Red and Blue," one of Penn's most iconic singing traditions. Klaus joined in and moved his arm back and forth across his chest to the words, "Hurrah! Hurrah! Pennsylvania!" along with everyone else. Kaihan wasn't even aware

Marge and Klaus on one of their many wonderful trips

that Klaus knew the words to that song since Klaus was not one for football games. The spontaneity of that moment is a good example of how central Penn was to his life.

Klaus and Marge shared many happy years together. They enjoyed the Philadelphia Orchestra, good movies, and lots of travel. Klaus was also very proud of Marge's own impressive career developments and intellectual projects. Marge admired him just as much, noting how incredibly prolific he was in the last thirty years of his life. He was the definitive word on content analysis, cybernetics, and product semantics, writing many well-received papers and books. Even in the hospital, about a month before he died, he gave a three-hour presentation from his bed, refusing to take a medical test he was supposed to have because he was presenting at a conference. The doctors, realizing how important it was, closed the door and wouldn't let anyone in the room until Klaus's meetings were over. Similarly, when hospital volunteers at Penn asked Klaus if he wanted to write a little essay or letter to his family, he opted to write a treatise on everything and discussed turning it into a book—about a week before he died! He entitled this piece *Metaphor: A Better Picture of the World* and it is included as an appendix in this book.

Family Time and Grandchildren

Family was one of the most important elements in Klaus's life. He made sure Kaihan and Heike had a strong connection with family in Germany and that they grew up knowing about their heritage by going to Europe almost yearly, including for multiple family reunions. He was always diligent in making sure that time and resources were spent evenly across all of the different family members, from Virginia to Connecticut to Europe.

The past twenty-plus years were all about the grandkids. Klaus was tremendously excited when he became a grandfather. Whenever a baby was due, he would try to be there for the birth. In fact, he even was in the delivery room for Heike's son Quinn's birth. It was an enormous event for him, and he was completely over the moon about each new baby. Klaus had seven grandchildren. From her own children, Marge had four, as well as one step-grandchild. Even Marge's grandkids called him Opa, and both Klaus and Marge treated all of the grandchildren on both sides of the family as their own.

Klaus and Marge would go to the grandkids' sports or school events; he loved being involved with their schools, like attending grandparents' day or UN day, when the kids would dress up under the Bangladesh or German flags. The kids would grab Klaus's and Marge's hands and walk the hallways, showing them each room, sitting in their classrooms. One year, Klaus was the volunteer Santa Claus for Marge's grandson Teddy's school. Teddy was still small so he was too scared to go sit on Santa's lap, but later he commented that "Santa sounded just like Opa."

Klaus played games with his grandchildren, too. Klaus would always bring with him a game or puzzle that he had thought of, or maybe a newspaper section from *The New York Times* for the kids. Marge would knit on the couch and Klaus would be on the floor playing board games with the kids. The kids knew that when Opa came to visit it would be board game time. He had a very childlike sense about him, which is perhaps where his creativity came from—so he loved getting on the floor. In fact, one time Klaus blew his hip out and spent Thanksgiving in the hospital, all from being on the ground playing games with the kids. Even in his eighties, you could find Klaus lying on his back side-by-side next to his son in the pouring rain at the Klaus House, trying to push a huge log off the road so the car could get by.

Marge and Klaus also traveled extensively, often with the kids: cruises to the Caribbean Islands, Mediterranean, Alaska, and the Norwegian coast to above the Arctic Circle and trips to Mexico, India, Australia, Belize, Israel, Jordan, Sweden, Singapore, Bali, and of course, Germany.

Remembering Klaus

Perhaps one of the best words to describe Klaus is "straightforward," in a literal and figurative sense. He never walked slowly or meandered; he walked with purpose, and it was all about getting from point A to point B. Heike remembers frequenting the Italian Market on weekends, trailing behind her dad while he strode ahead with his white canvas Land's End tote bag, hoping she wouldn't lose him.

Another time, he was pedaling Kaihan and Heike downtown on a bike, with Heike sitting on the handlebar and Kaihan in the back. As they parked the bike, another man came up to compliment Klaus: "It's amazing you can do that, I don't think I could." Klaus matter-of-factly replied, "Well, I guess some men are just stronger than other men." It wasn't meant to be rude—it was just an observation. So of course, Klaus was confused when the man got all puffed up and walked away!

Above all else, while Klaus was not particularly demonstrative, he was full of love for his family. This was very clear in how he interacted with his grandchildren, and he always found ways to show he cared. Perhaps with some influence from Marge, he started sending many letters on all kinds of holidays, from birthdays to Valentine's Day. He spoke about how proud he was of his children all the time. In his last days, he said to Marge, "My children, they're great, aren't they?"

Klaus and Heike at her marriage celebration

Klaus and Kaihan deep in discussion

Klaus, or Opa, and Marge with their grandchildren

Metaphor:
A Better Picture of the World

I want to write a small book
Of a foundational nature
With regard to language.
Over the last millennium,
People have had a misunderstanding of human nature,
And of determinism.
Aristotle and others had the idea
That everything is going in one direction:
Abstract forms come to Earth,
And everything is supposed to go in that direction.
This is called the logic of determinism.
This theory doesn't understand the nature of the process of speaking,
If one is understanding and thinking
That everything is coming from mathematics,
It is a false belief.
Math is a very powerful language that misguides.
Mathematics is spoken by mathematicians who have the freedom
Of defining any term that they like.

People speak with one another through metaphor.
It's complicated.
The simplest form to explain this is to say that
We talk about one thing in terms of another.
Metaphor connects experience with phenomena,
In the minds and experiences of people.
This is not a deterministic,

But a metaphorical,
Conception of language.

There are different ways of speaking,
And they have tremendously different implications
For everyday life.
Different languages have different effects.
For example, Fascism, interpersonal relationships,
Creative words and stories

All have different effects.
They are always understood within their language communities.

What we see now, with Trump, is the end of democracy.
It is important to critique language
And to understand who speaks for what purpose,
And what is dominant,
And what should be eliminated.
That is another element that has to do with Aristotle.
And with everything going in one direction.

In 1943 Norbert Weiner discovered cybernetics
As a control device.
Now we're stuck with this conception of the control
    of human beings,
Including their languages.
Cybernetics has its own language.
It has no space for metaphors.
Working with metaphorical forms
Gives a better picture of the world.

Curriculum Vitae
Klaus Krippendorff, PhD, PhD (h.c.)

Education
Ph.D. in Communications, University of Illinois, Urbana, 1967.
Dipl. Design, Ulm School of Design, Germany, 1961.
Ingenieur (grad.), State Engineering School Hanover, Germany, 1954.

Awards and Appointments

2017 Innovation Award for Methods from ICA's Mass communication Division

2016 Award "For his career achievements in CYBERNETICS APPLIED TO COMMUNICATION", from Business Systems Lab.

2016 Elected Fellow of the International Communicology Institute (ICI)

2016 Elected to the International Academy for Systems and Cybernetics Sciences (IASCYS)

2012 **Doctor of Philosophy** *honoris causa* from the Linnaeus University in Kalmar/Växjö, Sweden.

2012 "Article of the Year" award by the Communication Theory and Methodology division of AEJMC for http://repository.upenn.edu/asc_papers/278, in *Communication Methods & Measure 5*, 2: 1-20, 2011.

2012 Elected Fellow of the American Society for Cybernetics

2011 Member of Honorary Board of the World Complexity Science Academy

2011 Medal for contributions to understanding complex systems by the World Complexity Science Academy

2010-2022 **Emeritus Professor of Communication.** The Annenberg School for Communication, University of Pennsylvania

2001 Award of the Norbert Wiener Medal in Cybernetics in gold by the American Society for Cybernetics

2004 Award of the Norbert Wiener / Hermann Schmidt Prize by the German Society for Cybernetics, German Society for Pedagogy and Information, at the University of Vienna

2004 ICA Fellows Book Award for *Content Analysis; An Introduction to Its Methodology*

2000-2003 **Gregory Bateson Professor for Cybernetics, Language, and Culture,** University of Pennsylvania

1998 Named by graduate students as the teacher of the best doctorial course taken at the University of Pennsylvania
1998 (Fall) Visiting Professor, Musachino Art University, Tokyo, Japan. http://www.ssdsj.net/eng/
1998 Elected International Fellow of the Society for Science of Design Studies, Japan.
1994 (Spring) Visiting Professor, University of New Hampshire, Durham NH.
1993-2002 Member of the Graduate Group in Conflict Analysis and Peace Science
1993-94 Special Professor, University of the Arts, Philadelphia PA.
1992 1st Annual Jay Doblin Award for the best article published in *Design Management Journal*
1989-98 Member: National Advisory Board, Institute of Communication Research, Urbana/Champaign, IL
1988 Gordon Research Conference on Cybernetics, January 18-22, Oxnard, CA.
1986-87 Distinguished Visiting Professor, Ohio State University, Columbus, OH.
1985 Elected Fellow of the International Communication Association (ICA).
1984 Gordon Research Conference on Cybernetics, August 27-31, New Hampton, NH.
1982 Elected Fellow of the American Association for the Advancement of Science (AAAS).
1980-2010 **Professor of Communication,** The Annenberg School for Communication, University of Pennsylvania.
1979-80 Fellow, Netherlands Institute for Advanced Study in the Humanities and Social Sciences, Wassenaar.
1973 (Spring) Guest Professor, Interuniversitair Instituut Bedrijfskunde, Delft, Erasmus University Rotterdam, The Netherlands
1971 Award for "On Generating Data in Communication Research" as the most outstanding contribution to *The Journal of Communication* in 1970. http://repository.upenn.edu/asc_papers/273
1971 **Master of Arts *honoris causa*** from the University of Pennsylvania, Philadelphia.
1970-80 **Associate Professor,** The Annenberg School of Communications, University of Pennsylvania.
1970 (Summer) Guest Professor, Institut für Publizistik, Free University Berlin, Germany.

1967-86 Member of the Graduate Group of Social Systems Science at the University of Pennsylvania.
1966-70 **Assistant Professor,** The Annenberg School of Communications, University of Pennsylvania.
1965-66 Associate, The Annenberg School for Communication, University of Pennsylvania.
1964-65 Pre-doctoral Research Fellow, The Annenberg School of Communications, University of Pennsylvania.
1963-64 Research Assistant at the Institute for Communications Research, University of Illinois, Urbana.
1961-63 Ford International Fellow.
1961 Fulbright travel grant.
1961 Design award (for diploma work) by the Bundesverband der Deutschen Industrie.
1960-61 Research Assistant at the Institute for Visual Perception, Ulm School of Design, Germany.

Professional Involvements
Memberships:
   American Association for the Advancement of Science (AAAS)
   American Society for Cybernetics (ASC) (Fellow)
   Deutsche Gesellschaft für Publizistik und Kommunikationswissenschaft (DGPuK), (honorary)
   International Communication Association (ICA) (Life Member)
   International Society for Systems Science (ISSS)
   Institut für Kybernetik Berlin e.V.

Offices:
   Member of the Board of the Business Systems Laboratory. 2012-2022
   Member of the advisory Board of the World Complexity Science Academy. 2011-2022
   Member of the International Board of Economics & Business Knowledge. 2010-2022
   Trustee, American Society for Cybernetics (ASC), 1999-2008
   President and Founder of the International Federation of Communication Associations, 1991- 2008.
   President, International Communication Association (ICA), 1984-85.
   Board Member and Ombudsman, American Society for Cybernetics (ASC), 1980-83, 1991- 94.

   ASC Delegate to AAAS's Section T, Information, Computing and Communication, 1998- 2000.

ICA Delegate to AAAS's Section T, Information, Computing and Communication, 1978- 81.
Member at Large of ICA's Board of Directors, 1977-80.
Chair, Information Systems Division, Member of the Board of ICA, 1970-76.

Member of the editorial boards of:
Arcos Design – a Brazilian online journal 2009-2022
Artifact; Journal of Digital Design, 2003-2022
Communication and Information Science, 1986-2001;
Communication Methods and Measures, 2006-2022
Communication Monographs, 1985-1989;
Communication Research Reports 1985-2001;
Communication Research, 1974-1993;
Communication Studies, 2007-2022
Communication Theory, 1988-2004;
Communication Yearbook, 1977-1980, 1984-1989;
Communication, 1974-79;
Communications, The European Journal of Communication Research, 1985-2022;
Constructivist Foundations (an E-journal), 2004-2022
Cybernetics & Human Knowing, 1991-2022.
Electronic Journal of Communication, 2011-2022
Human Communication Research, 1977-80, 1985-89, 1998-2004.
Informatologia, 1991-2022;
Informatologia Yugoslavica, 1985-91;
International Journal of Cultural Studies, 1997-2008
International Journal of Markets and Business Systems, 2014-2022
Journal of Communication, 1984-92; 2002-10
Kybernetes, 2016-2022
Markets and Business Systems, 2015-2022
Sprache und Form, 2015-2022
The Radical Designist, 2016-2022

Reviewer for:
National Science Foundation (NSF)
Deutsche Forschungsgemeinschaft (DFG)
Entropy
Netherlands Institute for Advanced Studies (NIAS)
Israel Science Foundation
Swiss National Science Foundation (SNF)
Austrian Science Fund (FWF)
The American Scandinavian Foundation

Advances and Applications in Statistics
American Journal of Political Science
Behavioral Research Methods
Communication Methods and Measures
Communication Yearbook
Constructivist Foundations
Design Studies
Field Methods
International Journal of Communication
International Journal of Social Science Studies
Journal of the American Statistical Association
Journal for Peace Research
Journalism, Theory, Practice & Criticism
Management Communication Quarterly
Public Opinion Quarterly
Psychological Methods
Psychological Reports, Perceptual and Motor Skills
Sociological Methodology
The Information Society
The Sociological Quarterly
Quality and Quantity
Etc.

Activities:
    Gave three lectures in 2022 (Theories of Language Use; Cybernetics; and Content Analysis) and three workshops on Text Analysis on Zoom at Beijing Jiaotong University.

    Organized the symposium "Discourses in Action" for the Scholars Program in Culture and Communication at Annenberg School for Communication, University of Pennsylvania, December 2, 2016.

    Taught a two-day seminar on my *The Semantic Turn, a New Foundation for Design* at the University of Caldas, Manizales, Colombia. October 20-21, 2016.

    Taught a two-day workshop on advanced content analysis for European scholars at the University of Palermo, Italy. August 29-30, 2016.

    Presenter and organizer of a workshop on Human-Centered Design at the Universidad de Bogota Jorge Tadeo Lozano, 2011-11-20

One of two scientific coordinators of the 1st International Conference on Qualitative Research Methods at the University of Enna "Kore" in Sicily, 2011.9.1-3

Organizer of two workshops on Computer Applications in Content Analysis at ICA conferences in Acapulco, Mexico, 2001, and Washington, DC, 2002.

Co-organizer of an international workshop on "Semantics in Design and the Linguistic Nature of Things," München, Germany, February 18-20, 1998

Co-organizer of an NSF-sponsored Workshop on Design in the Age of Information. "design@1006.information.edu" Raleigh, NC: North Carolina State University, February 29 – March 3, 1996. http://repository.upenn.edu/asc_papers/96

Co-organizer of the International Conference on "Cybernetics in the Art of Learning" for the American Society for Cybernetics, Philadelphia, November 1993.

Co-organizer of a Workshop and First European Symposium on Product Semantics, Helsinki, Finland, May 1989.

Co-organizer of a one-week workshop on Product Semantics at Corporate Design, Philips, Eindhoven. July 1985.

Co-organizer of a Workshop on Product Semantics for the Industrial Designers Society of America (IDSA) at the Cranbrook Academy of Art, August 1984.

Organizer of the International Communication Association (ICA) Conference on "Communication in Transition," ICA Conference, San Francisco, May 1984.

Organizer of the National Conference on "Communication and Control Processes in Society," Philadelphia, October-November 1974.

Co-Organizer of the National Conference on "Content Analysis," Philadelphia, November 1967.

Participant, presenter of papers, or organizer of symposia at meetings of the:
- Aalto University, School of Arts and Design in Helsinki
- Alta Conference (Utah)
- American Association for the Advancement of Science (AAAS)
- American Society for Cybernetics (ASC): http://www.youtube.com/watch?v=nK8O9ZxyIaE
- Annenberg School for Communications, University of Southern California: http://www.youtube.com/watch?v=5CUs0NtFpIs
- Association for Education in Journalism and Mass Communication (AEJMC)
- Cooper-Hewitt, National Design Museum, a Smithonian Institution, New York Conference on Writing across the Curriculum (WAC)
- Congresso Brasileiro de Pesquisa & Desenvolimento em Design.
- Design Management Institute
- Deutsche Gesellschaft für Publizistik und Kommunikationswissenschaft (DGPuK)
- Deutsche Gesellschaft für Semiotics
- East-West Center, Honolulu, Hawaii
- European Communication Association (ECA)
- Gordon Research Conference
- Industrial Designer Society of America (IDSA)
- Interaction Design Association (IxDA): http://vimeo.com/album/2488675/video/86240674
- International Association for Dialogue Analysis
- International Association for Mass Communication Research (IAMCR) International Congress for Cybernetics and Systems Research
- International Communication Association (ICA)
- International Society for the Systems Sciences (ISSS)
- Issues in Nursing Research Conference
- Konstfack, University College of Arts, Crafts and Design, Stockholm, Sweden: http://vimeo.com/43316950
- Linnaeus University, Kalmar, Sweden
- Middle East Technical University in Ankara, Turkey
- Netherlands Institute for Advanced Studies (NIAS)
- Society for Science of Design Studies, Japan

- Speech Communication Association/National Communication Association (NCA)
- Temple Conference on Culture and Communication

Temple Conference on Discourse Analysis
Universidad de Bogota Jorge Tadeo Lozano
Universität der Künste, Berlin, Germany (UdK)
World Complexity Science Academy (WCSA):
   http://www.youtube.com/watch?v=EbqcYbjFK8U
Zentrum für Kunst und Medien, Karlsruhe

Scholarly Interests
- Critical cybernetics – An emancipatory discourse addressing epistemological pathologies in society.
- Qualitative methods and discursive constructions of reality – discourse and conversation analysis.
- Constructivist Epistemology and discursive (second-order) cybernetics.
- Critical analyses of scientific discourses
- Mathematical foundations of cybernetics, general systems, communication and information theories.
- Methodology of communication research; Analysis, critique and development of qualitative and quantitative techniques for empirical inquiry; Semantic analyses of ethnographic data.
- Content Analysis: Theory of content and practical content analyses; Critique of existing empirical techniques and development of new computational methods
- Disagreement and reliability analysis (various versions of Krippendorff's α).
- Critical Scholarship; Attempts to develop conceptions and methods of inquiry into social phenomena that reveal possibilities for change rather than describe what was; Liberating concepts, writing, and languaging especially in respect for Others.
- Design: Theory of product semantics; Human-centered and culture-sensitive design; Research for human-computer interface design: telephone, computer-supported cooperation and special applications; Design principles for the information age.

Graduate Courses:
Discursive Constructions of Realities (formally Language and Social Constructions of Realities). An inquiry into the principles and processes by which realities come to be socially constructed, linguistically institutionalized, and discursively maintained. This seminar serves as an introduction to qualitative inquiry into the emerging epistemology of communication. It provides students with dialogical and discursive tools to inquire into the histories and cultural differences of various social

phenomena. It favors a reflexive/ethnographic approach that involves entering one's cognition into the sociology one comes to construct in the cause of observation and action. It explores the artifacts that discourses create, including scientific theories, models, and ideologies. In such explorations, students learn to boldly challenge all kinds of taken-for-granted realities, asking why some of them tend to hide their constructedness, and if experienced as burdensome or oppressive, probing into possibilities of liberation from them. The seminar is committed to critical scholarship and emancipatory pursuits, which are allied with feminist writing, cultural studies, and reflexive social inquiries.

Cybernetics, Systems and Media, earlier Models of Communication. An introduction to cybernetics and systems theory, whose concepts are fueling the present information-technological revolution. Students become acquainted with the formal building blocks for constructing models of communication and complex systems, whether these concern causal, cognitive, or social phenomena; with various theories of human interfaces with technology: cyborg, information, autopoietic, and coordination theories; and with second- order cybernetics, which offers a reflexive approach to understanding. The interdisciplinary scope of the course enables students to draw on knowledge from a diversity of empirical domains.

Cybernetics and Society. Models of communication and control are applied to various social phenomena and contrasted with other conceptual frameworks in the social sciences. Among the conceptions that are developed are those of information networks; recursions a system as contrasted with the exertion of influence; feedback (recursion and teleology); autopoiesis, self-organization, self-observing systems and other forms of recursive networks of interaction; natural, social, and artificial intelligence; different manifestations of natural selection/ ultra-stability in perception, cognition, self-repair, and immune systems; chaos theory.

Information in Qualitative Data. The course develops multi-variate methods for exploring a variety of qualitative data and simultaneously broadens concepts of information and communication in a variety of social settings. While qualitative data are common in social research, their systematic analysis has been largely neglected. Recent developments have facilitated the use of qualitative data as a source of insights. The use of information theory as a vehicle for exploration is particularly appealing to communication researchers in search of new theoretical perspectives.

Semantics of Communication. Most social inquiries rely on linguistic data: written documents, letters, interview transcripts, field notes or published reports. The sole reason for their being is the meanings they have for particular readers. This course considers various theories of meanings, how texts are used, by whom, and in which institutional settings; and it explores the methods of analysis that these theories inform. It introduces several qualitative research traditions, presents case studies, and reviews the concepts, logic, and analytical models needed for independent qualitative research. The course is ethnographic in its approach to data collection (interviews, observational accounts, written matter); analytical in the way it probes its data (with models drawn largely from cultural anthropology); qualitative in the empirical methods it encourages (metaphor, conversation, and discourse analysis); dialogic in its respect for multiple voices (as opposed to the more familiar monologue); and critical or emancipatory in the consequences it aspires to.

Content Analysis. An introduction to the analysis of large bodies of textual matter: content analysis, also called message systems analysis, quantitative semantics, propaganda analysis, text analysis, or an approach to big communication data. The course inquires into the methods, empirical problems, and theories underlying these analytical efforts: sampling, text retrieval, coding, reliability, analytical constructs, computational techniques, and inferences. It demonstrates these with studies of mass media content, interview or panel data, and systematic efforts to provide legal evidence or draw valid inferences from personal documents or electronic exchanges. Students learn to design a content analysis and do the preliminary work on it. They may also perform a content analysis on already available data, develop a new analytical technique from available theories and test it, or they may explore relevant literature to solve a methodological problem in content analysis.

Seminar in Message Analysis. Advanced topics in the analysis of verbal and non-verbal message content will be considered and methodological or practical problems arising out of research projects will be solved in a seminar format. Among the topics that might be considered are: experiments with recording qualitative data, expansion of the system of agreement analysis, further formalization of data languages, attempts at validation, development of new analytical techniques and computer aided text analysis procedures, analytical use of available theories of cognition and symbolic behavior, exploration of systems that could integrate the results of different kinds of empirical research techniques with content analysis findings.

Undergraduate Courses:

Language in the Social Construction of Realities. Departing from traditional notions of language as a medium, this course sheds light on the discursive practices that constitute the realities we come to live in and observe. Readings and lectures develop the concepts needed to understand how realities are socially constructed or 'languaged' into being. Seminar-like discussions and individual students' contributions offer opportunities to critically examine a variety of constructions of reality from this perspective: facts, emotions, social problems, race, gender, hegemony, family, science, technology, and more. Students learn to appreciate how their own identity and their own world is shaped by the language they use. They take with them analytical skills and practical abilities to alter if not the way social reality is constructed so at least their own participation in it.

Social Cybernetics. Basic ideas about communication in society are explored from a cybernetic and systems theoretical perspective. The course acknowledges the traditional assumptions of linearity (communication as an intentional and one-way process) but builds on the recognition that most social processes are circular, emerging, self-sustaining, and controlling their own destiny. It starts with simple circularities, such as feedback, moves through the biological idea of autopoiesis (the ability of living systems to create and maintain their own boundary while organizing themselves within it) to self-organizing social systems. Principles of information generation, processing, storing, and communication are discussed. Evolutionary aspects of cultural artifacts, such as rituals, and of technological systems are explored. The lives of large communication networks are examined, and paradigms of self-observing systems are developed.

Human-centered Design. The word "design" derives from "de + signare," to "mark," "to make things into signs" or to make them meaningful to their users. Starting with the axiom that humans do not respond to the physics of things but to what they mean to them, the course explores how artifacts, especially language-like or intelligent ones, constitute themselves in various social practices and in their users' understanding.

Key to this approach is the recognition that artifacts are understandable only through their interfaces and that human-centered design, as opposed to engineering or the design of functions has to address these.
- The course distinguishes four contexts in which artifacts must survive: use, language, ontogenesis, and the ecology of other artifacts.
- It develops a vocabulary, a language, to empirically study and describe a variety of meanings – a semantics – for each context in which artifacts must survive in interaction with different stakeholders, including among designers who too have a stake in the viability of their designs.
- It develops methods for designing artifacts that are culture-sensitive and respect what users or more generally stakeholders can make sense of and learn in their respective domains of experiences.
- And it develops empirical tests to validate the semantic claims that designers need to make to those who could bring their design to fruition.

From Conversation to Discourse, lecture at the Annenberg School for Communication and Journalism at the University of Southern California, October 10, 2011. https://www.asc.upenn.edu/news- events/annenberg-video/faculty-videos/klaus-krippendorff-lecture-annenberg-west

Discussion of key concepts in his *The Semantic Turn; A New Foundation for Design,* at the Konstfack in Stockholm, 2012. https://www.asc.upenn.edu/news-events/annenberg-video/faculty-videos/professor- klaus-krippendorff-discusses-key-concepts

Five interviews of Klaus Krippendorff at his home, conducted by Jeff Pooley as part of the oral history project of the Annenberg Library Archive, The Annenberg School of Communication, University of Pennsylvania.

1st on December 20th, 2016   https://vimeo.com/198725732
2nd on January 18th, 2017   https://vimeo.com/200237170
3rd on February 22nd, 2017   https://vimeo.com/205610302
4th on April 12th, 2017   https://vimeo.com/214223618
5th on May 17th, 2017   https://vimeo.com/218011456

A Podcast
About the first chapter of my Semantic Turn, put together at the

Ostbayerische Technische Hochschule, Regensburg, Germany in a seminar on Design Theory, Summer Semester 2019 taught by Prof. Dr. Rosan Chow, and visualized by 4th. semester students: Alicia Lindner, Andrea Florea, Bianca Spronraft, Gian van Rooyen & Patricia Lang.
https://vimp.oth-regensburg.de/video/The-Semantic-Turn-/53e78d919c5fd75bf94cae72c2bb2ead

Publications:

Books and Monographs

The Chinese translation of the 4th edition of Content Analysis in progress by Li Ming of the School of Journalism & Communication, Nanjing University for Tsinghua University Press in Beijing – in process.

The Reliability of Generating Data.
Abingdon, UK: Chapman and Hall/CRC press, 2023.

Content Analysis; An Introduction to Its Methodology, 4th Edition.
Thousand Oaks, CA: Sage, 2019.

Chinese translation by Prof. Dr. Fei Hu of
The Semantic Turn; A New Foundation for Design. Beijing: China Architecture & Building Press, 2017.

Chinese translation by Tommy Cho, Ph.D.
Content Analysis; An Introduction to Its Methodology 3rd Edition; 488 pages. Taipei, Taiwan: Wunan Publishing Co, 2014.

German translation of
The Semantic Turn; A New Foundation for Design:
Die semantische Wende. Eine neue Grundlage für Design. Schriften zur Gestaltung / Züricher Hochschule der Künste. R. Michel (Ed.). Basel: Birkhäuser Verlag/ De Gruyter, 2013.

Content Analysis; An Introduction to Its Methodology 3rd Edition; 441 pages. Thousand Oaks, CA: Sage Publications, 2013. Replacement of Section 12.4 to be introduced into its 4th edition. http://www.asc.upenn.edu/usr/krippendorff/U-alpha.pdf

Japanese Translation of
The Semantic Turn; A New Foundation for Design
394 pages. Tokyo: SIBaccess Co. Ltd. 2009.

On Communicating; Otherness, Meaning, and Information.
Fernando Bermejo (Ed.). New York: Routledge, 2009.

The Semantic Turn; A New Foundation for Design.
Boca Raton, London, New York: Taylor & Francis CRC, 2006.

Content Analysis; An Introduction to Its Methodology, 2nd Edition.
413 pages. Thousand Oaks, CA: Sage publications, 2019. https://www.academia.edu/36602778/Second_Edition_Content_Ana lysis?email_work_card=reading-history

A Tartalomelemzés Módszertanának Alapjai.
Budapest: Balassi Kiad, 1995. Hungarian translation of *Content Analysis; An Introduction to its Methodology*

Design: A Discourse on Meaning; A Work Book. Philadelphia, PA: University of the Arts, Summer 1994.

Analisis isi: Pengantar teori dan metodologi.
Terjemahan Farid Wajidi, (Tr.). Jakarta: Rajawali Press, 1991. Indonesian translation of Content Analysis; *An Introduction to its Methodology.*

Metodologia de análisis de contenido: Teoria y practica. Barcelona-Buenos Aires-Mexico: Ediciones Paidos, 1990.
Spanish translation of *Content Analysis; An Introduction to its Methodology.*

Japanese translation of a revised version of
Content Analysis; An Introduction to its Methodology. Tokyo: Keiso Communication, 1990.

Farsi translation by Houshang Nayebi of
Content Analysis; An Introduction to its Methodology. Tehran: NEY, 1988.

Information Theory: Structural Models for Qualitative Data; 96 pages.
Beverly Hills, CA: Sage Publications, 1986.

A Dictionary of Cybernetics.
Norfolk, VA: The American Society for Cybernetics, 1986. http://repository.upenn.edu/asc_papers/224
Entrees also available on: http://pespmc1.vub.ac.be/ASC/INDEXASC.html

Analisi del Contenuto; Introduzione Methodologica. Introduzione di Enzo Campelli. Torino: ERI, 1983.
Italian translation of *Content Analysis; An Introduction to its Methodology.*

Content Analysis; An Introduction to its Methodology. Beverly Hills, CA: Sage, 1980.

An Examination of Content Analysis: A Proposal for a Framework and an Information Calculus for Message Analytic Situations. 400 pages. Ph.D. Dissertation. Urbana: University of Illinois, 1967.
http://repository.upenn.edu/asc_papers/250/

Über den Zeichen- und Symbolcharakter von Gegenständen: Versuch zu einer Zeichentheorie für die Programmierung von Produktformen in sozialen Kommunikationsstrukturen. 138 pages. Diploma Thesis. Hochschule für Gestaltung, Ulm, 1961. http://repository.upenn.edu/asc_papers/233

Discourses in Action; What Language Enables Us to Do.
Edited with Nour Halabi.
New York: Routledge/Taylor & Francis, 2020.

The Content Analysis Reader. Edited with Mary Angela Bock. 481 pages. Thousand Oaks, CA: Sage Publications, 2009.

Design in the Age of Information;
A Report to the National Science Foundation (NSF). Edited. 184 pages. Raleigh, NC: Design Research Laboratory, School of Design, North Carolina State University, 1997.
 http://repository.upenn.edu/asc_papers/96

Special issue devoted to Product Semantics. Edited with Reinhart Butter. 140 pages. *Design Issues 5,* 2, 1989.

Special issue devoted to Product Semantics, Edited with Reinhart Butter. 36 pages. *Innovations 3,* 2, 1984.

Special issue devoted to Autopoiesis. Co-edited with Milan Zeleny. 39 pages. *Cybernetic Forum 10,* 2&3, 1981.

Communication and Control in Society. Edited. 597 pages. New York: Gordon and Breach, 1979.

The Analysis of Communication Content; Developments in Scientific Theories and Computer Techniques. Edited with George Gerbner, Ole R. Holsti, William J. Paisley & Philip J. Stone.
529 pages. New York: John Wiley & Sons, 1969.

Book Chapters
Krippendorff's Alpha. Pp.767-772 in *The SAGE Encyclopedia of Research Design, 2nd Ed.* Bruce B. Frey (Ed.). Los Angeles, CA. ...: SAGE reference. 2022.

Communication, Conversation, Discourse and Design. Pp.21-36 in *Matters of Communication;* Formen und Materialitäten gestalteter Kommunikation. Sabine Foraita, Bianca Herlo & Axel Vogelsang (Eds.) Deutsche Gesellschaft für Designtheorie und -forschung, Bielefeld, Germany: Transcript Verlag 2020.
https://repository.upenn.edu/asc_papers/821

Design Discourse. Pp. 333-341 in Thilo Schwer & Kai Vöckler (Eds.). *Der Offenbacher Ansatz – Zur Theorie der Produktsprache.* Bielefeld, Germany: Transcript Verlag, 2020. https://repository.upenn.edu/asc_papers/820

Design Muss Sinn Machen (1986). Pp. 269-283 in Thilo Schwer & Kai Vöckler (Eds.). *Der Offenbacher Ansatz – Zur Theorie der Produktsprache.* Bielefeld, Germany: Transcript Verlag, 2020.

Why discourses in action? Chinese Translation by Hailong Tian of Klaus Krippendorff's Introduction to Krippendorff & Halabi (Eds.) (2020). *Discourses in Action; What Language Enables Us to Do.* Contemporary Rhetoric 221, 5: 46-55, 2020. https://repository.upenn.edu/asc_papers/827

Why discourses in action? An Introduction. Pp.1-13 in K. Krippendorff & N. Halabi (Eds.). Discourses in Action; What Language Enables Us to Do. New York: Routledge/Taylor & Francis, 2020.

"Relying on accountability to challenge authority, agency, and power" and "Extending accountability to scholarly accounts of authority" – Two contributions to Chapter 4, pp. 56-76 in N. Bencherki, F. Matte & F. Cooren (Eds.). *Authority and Power in Social Interaction: Methods and Analysis*. New York: Routledge/Taylor & Francis, 2020.

The Cybernetics of Design and the Design of Cybernetics. Pp. 119– 136 in Thomas Fisher & Christiane M. Herr (Eds.). *Design Cybernetics – Navigating the New*. Berlin: Springer Verlag, 2019.

Discourses in the Design of Cultural Artifacts. Pp. 77 – 111 in M. Freise (Ed.). *Inspired by Bakhtin. Dialogical Methods in the Humanities*. Series on Studies in Comparative Literature and Intellectual History. G. Tihanov (Ed.). Brighton, MA: Academic Studies Press, 2018.

A Professor's Perspective on 50 Years. Pp. 178-179 in Anne Sceia Klein & Vilma Barr (Eds.). *On the Cusp; The Women of Penn '64*. Medford, NJ: Pine Road Press, 2018.

Reliability. Pp. 1591-1618 in Jörg Matthes (Ed.). *The International Encyclopedia of Communication Research Methods*. Hoboken, NJ: Wiley-Blackwell, 2017.

Intercoder Reliability Coefficients, Comparisons of. Pp. 724 – 729 in M. Allen (Ed.). The SAGE Encyclopedia of Communication Research Methods. Thousand Oaks, CA: Sage, 2018.

Intercoder Reliability Techniques: Krippendorff's Alpha. Pp. 743 – 750 in M. Allen (Ed.). The SAGE Encyclopedia of Communication Research Methods. Thousand Oaks, CA: Sage, 2017.

Design, an Undisciplinable Profession. Pp. 124, 197-206, in G. Joost, K. Bredies, M. Christensen, F. Conradi & A. Unteidig (Eds.). *Design as Research. Positions, Arguments, Perspectives*. Basel: Birkhäuser Verlag/De Gruyter (2016) https://repository.upenn.edu/asc_papers/628

Data. Pp. 484-489 in K. Brun-Jensen & R. T. Craig (Eds.). *International Encyclopedia of Communication Theory and Philosophy*. Hoboken, NJ: Wiley-Blackwell and ICA. 2016. (ISBN 9781118766804).

Design. Pp. 515-527 in K. Brun-Jensen, R. T. Craig (Eds.). *International Encyclopedia of Communication Theory and Philosophy*. Hoboken, NJ: Wiley-Blackwell and ICA. 2016. (ISBN 9781118766804) https://repository.upenn.edu/asc_papers/825

Social constructions of reality. Pp. 1874-1882 in K. Brun-Jensen & R. T. Craig (Eds.), *International Encyclopedia of Communication Theory and Philosophy*. Hoboken, NJ: Wiley-Blackwell and ICA. 2016. (ISBN 9781118766804).

Cybernetics. Pp. 135–136, in W. Donsbach (Ed.). *The Concise Encyclopedia of Communication*. Blackwell Publishing Ltd. 2015.

Information. Pp. 254 – 255, in W. Donsbach (Ed.). *The Concise Encyclopedia of Communication*. Blackwell Publishing Ltd. 2015.

Reliability. Pp. 529–530, in W. Donsbach (Ed.). *The Concise Encyclopedia of Communication*. Blackwell Publishing Ltd. 2015.

Validity. Pp. 637–638, in W. Donsbach (Ed.). The Concise Encyclopedia of Communication. Blackwell Publishing Ltd. 2015.

Designing Design-forsch-ung: not Re-search. Pp. 106-117 in Daniel Klapsing, et al. (Eds.). z.B. Weimar: Verlag der BauhausUniversität Weimar, 2013.

Cybernetics as discourse. Pp. 434-451 in Věra Barandovská-Frank Ed.). Littera Scripta Manet, Serta in Honorem Helmar Frank. Paderborn/Prag: Academia Libroservo. 2013.

Representation, Re-presentation, Presentation, and Conversation. Pp. 143-159 in François Cooren & Alain Létourneau (Eds.). *(Re)presentations and Dialogue*. Amsterdam/Philadelphia: John Benjamins, 2012.

Conversation and its erosion into discourse and computation. Pp. 129-174 in Torkild Thellefsen, Brent Sørensen & Paul Cobley (Eds.). *From First to Third via Cybernetics*. Fredericksberg, Denmark: SL forlagene, 2011. http://repository.upenn.edu/asc_papers/283.

Discourse and the Materiality of Its Artifacts. Chapter 2, pp. 23-46 in Timothy R. Kuhn (Ed.). *Matters of Communication: Political, Cultural, and Technological Challenges to Communication Theorizing*. New York: Hampton Press, 2011. http://repository.upenn.edu/asc_papers/259 Translated into French: Le discours et la matérialité de ses artefacts. Communication & Languages 2012 (173): 17-42.

Four (In)Determinabilities, Not One. Chapter 14, pp. 315-344 in Jose V. Ciprut (Ed.). *Indeterminacy: The Mapped, the Navigable, and the Uncharted*. Cambridge, MA: MIT Press, 2009. http://repository.upenn.edu/asc_papers/239

Mathematical Theory of Communication. Pp. 614-618 in S. W. Littlejohn & K. A. Foss (Eds). *Encyclopedia of Communication Theory*. Los Angeles, CA: Sage, 2009. http://repository.upenn.edu/asc_papers/169

Cybernetics. Pp. 285-290 in S. W. Littlejohn & K. A. Foss (Eds). *Encyclopedia of Communication Theory*. Los Angeles, CA: Sage, 2009.

Designing In Ulm and off Ulm. Pp. 55-72 in Karl-Achim Czember (Ed.). *HfG, Ulm; Die Abteilung Produktgestaltung; 39 Rückblicke*. Dortmund, Germany: Verlag Dorothea Rohn, 2008. http://repository.upenn.edu/asc_papers/138

Cybernetics. Pp. 1152-1159 in Wolfgang Donsbach (Ed.). *The International Encyclopedia of Communication, Vol. V*. Oxford, UK and Malden, MA: Wiley-Blackwell, 2008. http://gaiapc.ca/PJ/Cybernetics.pdf

Generalizability. Pp. 1951-1954 in Wolfgang Donsbach (Ed.). *The International Encyclopedia of Communication Vol. V*. Oxford, UK and Malden, MA: Wiley-Blackwell, 2008.

Information. Pp. 2213-2221 in Wolfgang Donsbach (Ed.). *The International Encyclopedia of Communication Vol. V*. Oxford, UK and Malden, MA: Wiley-Blackwell, 2008.

Reliability. Pp. 4174-4179 in Wolfgang Donsbach (Ed.). *The International Encyclopedia of Communication Vol. V*. Oxford, UK and Malden, MA: Wiley-Blackwell, 2008.

Systems Theory. Pp. 4941-4943 in Wolfgang Donsbach (Ed.). *The International Encyclopedia of Communication Vol. V.* Oxford, UK and Malden, MA: Wiley-Blackwell, 2008.

Validity. Pp. 5245-5251 in Wolfgang Donsbach (Ed.). *The International Encyclopedia of Communication Vol. V.* Oxford, UK and Malden, MA: Wiley-Blackwell, 2008.

Design Research; an Oxymoron? Pp. 67-80 in Ralf Michel (Ed.). *Design Research Now; Essays and Selected Projects.* Zürich: Birkhäuser Verlag, 2007. http://repository.upenn.edu/asc_papers/45

With Reinhart Butter, Semantics: Meanings and Contexts of Artifacts. Pp. 353-376 in H. N. J. Schifferstein & P. Hekkert (Eds.). *Product experience.* New York: Elsevier, 2008. http://repository.upenn.edu/asc_papers/91

The Social Construction of Public Opinion. Pp. 129-149 in Edith Wienand; Joachim Westerbarkey; and Armin Scholl (Eds.). *Kommunikation über Kommunikation. Theorie, Methoden und Praxis.* Festschrift für Klaus Merten. Wiesbaden, Germany: VS-Verlag, 2005. http://repository.upenn.edu/asc_papers/75/

Writing: Monologue, Dialogue, and Ecological Narrative. Pp. 119-159 in Michael B. Hinner (Ed.), *Introduction to Business Communication.* Freiberger Beiträge zur interkulturellen und Wirtschaftskommunikation, Band 1. Frankfurt: Peter Lang, 2005. http://repository.upenn.edu/asc_papers/93

Design Discourse: A Way to Redesign Design (Keynote Address to the Society for the Science of Design Studies, Japan, 2000), in English, pp. 01.5 – 01.11; in Japanese, pp. 01.12 -- 01.20; Special Issue: *Reconstruction of Meaning in Design and Next Dimensions of Design,* Japanese Society for the Science of Design, Tokyo, 2002.
http://repository.upenn.edu/asc_papers/227

Foreword, Pp. xvii-xix in Herminia C. M. Alfonso, *Socially Shared Inquiry; A self-Reflexive Emancipatory Communication Approach to Social Re-search.* Sikatuna Village, Quezon City, Philippines: Great Books Trading. 2001.

Propositions of Human-centeredness: A Philosophy for Design. Pp. 55-63 in David Durling & Ken Friedman (Eds.), *Doctoral Education in Design: Foundations for the Future*. Staffordshire (UK): Staffordshire University Press, 2000. http://repository.upenn.edu/asc_papers/210 in https://www.academia.edu/11320895/Durling_and_Friedman._2000._La_Clusaz_Proceedings_Doctoral_Ed ucation_in_Design.

Ecological Narratives: Reclaiming the Voice of Theorized Others. Chapter 1, pp. 1-26, in Jose V. Ciprut (Ed.). *The Art of the Feud; Reconceptualizing International Relations*. Westport, CT: Praeger Publishers, 2000. http://repository.upenn.edu/asc_papers/97/

On the Otherness that Theory Creates. Chapter 1, pp. 1-13 in Jose V. Ciprut (Ed.). *Of Fears and Foes; Security and Insecurity in an Evolving Global Political Economy*. Westport, CT: Praeger Publishers, 2000. http://repository.upenn.edu/asc_papers/296

A Field for Growing Doctorates in Design? Pp. 207-224 in R. Buchanan, et al. (Eds.), *Doctoral Education in Design 1998; Proceedings of the Ohio State Conference*. Pittsburgh, PA: School of Design, Carnegie Mellon University, 1999. http://repository.upenn.edu/asc_papers/241

Principales metáforas de la comunicación y algunas reflexiones constructivistas acerca de su utilización. Chapter 4, pp. 107-146 in Marcelo Pakman (Ed.). *Construcciones de la Experiencia Humana II*. Barcelona, Spain: Gedisa editorial, 1997. http://repository.upenn.edu/asc_papers/333

A Trajectory of Artificiality and New Principles of Design for the Information Age. Pp. 91-95 in Klaus Krippendorff (Ed.), *Design in the Age of Information, A Report to the National Science Foundation (NSF)*. Raleigh, NC: Design Research Laboratory, School of Design, North Carolina State University, 1997. http://repository.upenn.edu/asc_papers/95

Seeing Oneself through Others' Eyes in Social Inquiry. Chapter 2, pp. 47-72 in Michael Huspeck & Gary P. Radford (Eds.). *Transgressing Discourses; Communication and the Voice of Other*. Albany, NY: SUNY Press, 1997.
On the Reliability of Unitizing Continuous Data. Chapter 2, pp. 47-76 in Peter V. Marsden (Ed.). *Sociological Methodology*, 1995, Vol. 25. Cambridge, MA: Blackwell, 1995. 7 DOI:10.2307/271061

Redesigning Design; An Invitation to a Responsible Future. Pp. 138-162 in Päivi Tahkokallio & Susann Vihma (Eds.) Design - *Pleasure or Responsibility?* Helsinki: University of Art and Design, 1995. http://repository.upenn.edu/asc_papers/46

The Past of Communication's Hoped-For Future. Pp. 42-52 in Mark R. Levy & Michael Gurevich (Eds.). *Defining Media Studies; Reflections on the Future of the Field.* New York: Oxford University Press, 1994. https://repository.upenn.edu/asc_papers/532
(Originally Journal of Communication 43, 3: 34-44, 1993).

A Recursive Theory of Communication. Pp. 78-104 in David Crowley and David Mitchell (Eds.). *Communication Theory Today.* Cambridge, UK: Polity Press, 1994. http://repository.upenn.edu/asc_papers/209

Der Verschwundene Bote; Metaphern und Modelle der Kommunikation. Pp. 79-113 in Klaus Merten, Siegfried J. Schmidt & Siegfried Weischenberg (Eds.) *Die Wirklichkeit der Medien; Eine Einführung in die Kommunikationswissenschaft.* Opladen, Germany: Westdeutscher Verlag, 1994. http://repository.upenn.edu/asc_papers/258

Two Paths in Search of (the) Meaning (of Things). Pp. 113-142 in Michael Titzmann (Ed.). *Zeichen(theorie) in der Praxis.* Passau, Germany: Wissenschaftsverlag Rothe, 1993. http://repository.upenn.edu/asc_papers/256

Schritte zu einer konstruktivistischen Erkenntnistheorie der Massenkommunikation (G. Bentele & M. Rühl, transl.), pp. 19-51. Commentary by Klaus Merten, Horst Reimann, Lutz Erbring and Ulrich Saxer, pp. 52-73. In Günter Bentele and Manfred Rühl (Eds.). *Theorien Öffentlicher Kommunikation.* München, Germany: Ölschlaeger, 1993. http://repository.upenn.edu/asc_papers/293

Transcending Semiotics; Toward Understanding Design for Understanding. Pp. 24-47 in Susann Vihma (Ed.) *Objects and Images; Studies in Design and Advertising.* Helsinki: University of Industrial Arts, 1992. http://repository.upenn.edu/asc_papers/295

Reconstructing (some) Communication Research Methods. Chapter 7, pp. 115-142 in Frederic Steier (Ed.). *Research and Reflexivity.* London, England: Sage, 1991.

Product Semantics: A Triangulation and Four Design Theories. Pp. a3-a23 in Seppo Väkevä (Ed.). *Product Semantics '89*. Helsinki, Finland: University of Industrial Arts, 1990. http://repository.upenn.edu/asc_papers/254

Models and Metaphors of Communication. Manuscript for a textbook chapter and radio program for an educational series "Media and Communication, Construction of Realities" published, translated, and aired by Hessischer Rundfunk, Frankfurt, Germany, 1990. Published as: Der verschwundene Bote; Metaphern und Modelle der Kommunikation. Studienbrief 3: 11-50. *Medien und Kommunikation, Konstruktionen von Wirklichkeiten*. Weinheim & Basel: Beltz Verlag, 1990. http://repository.upenn.edu/asc_papers/276

Content Analysis. Pp. 403-407 in Erik Barnouw et al. (Ed.). *International Encyclopedia of Communication*, Vol. 1. New York: Oxford University Press, 1989. http://repository.upenn.edu/asc_papers/226

Cybernetics. Pp. 443-446 in Erik Barnouw et al. (Ed.). *International Encyclopedia of Communications*, Vol. 1. New York: Oxford University Press, 1989. http://repository.upenn.edu/asc_papers/211

Information Theory. Pp. 314-320 in Erik Barnouw et al. (Ed.). *International Encyclopedia of Communication*, Vol 2. New York: Oxford University Press, 1989. http://repository.upenn.edu/asc_papers/212

Shannon, Claude. Pp. 58-61 in Erik Barnouw et al. (Ed.). *International Encyclopedia of Communications*, Vol. 4. New York: Oxford University Press, 1989. http://repository.upenn.edu/asc_papers/213

On the Ethics of Constructing Communication. Presidential address delivered at the International Communication Association Conference on Paradigm Dialogues, Honolulu, Hawaii, May 26, 1985. Chapter 4, pp. 66-96 in Brenda Dervin, Larry Grossberg, Barbara J. O'Keefe and Ellen Wartella (Eds.). *Rethinking Communication: Paradigm Issues, Vol .I.* Newbury Park, CA: Sage, 1989.
http://repository.upenn.edu/asc_papers/275

Zum Kontext des Artefakts. Pp. 256-279 in R. Komar & I. Antoni (Eds.). Gestaltung und Wirklichkeit. Stuttgart: Deutsche Verlagsanstalt, 1989.

A Heretic Communication about Communication about Communication about Reality. Keynote address presented at the 40th Anniversary of the Institute of Communication Research, University of Illinois, Urbana-Champaign, March 18-19, 1988. Chapter 10, pp. 257-276, in Miriam Campanella (Ed.). *Between Rationality and Cognition*. Turin and Geneva: Albert Meynier, 1988. http://repository.upenn.edu/asc_papers/235

Paradigms for Communication and Development with Emphasis on Autopoiesis. Chapter 14, pp. 189-208 in D. Lawrence Kincaid (Ed.). *Communication Theory: Eastern and Western Perspectives*. New York: Academic Press, 1987.

Produktsemantik. Pp. 58-69 in Martin Krampen & Horst Kächele (Eds.). *Umwelt, Gestaltung und Persönlichkeit; Reflexionen 30 Jahre nach der Gründung der Ulmer Hochschule für Gestaltung*. Hildesheim, Germany: Georg Olms, 1986. http://repository.upenn.edu/asc_papers/292

Paradox and Information. Chapter 2, in Brenda Dervin & Melvin J. Voigt (Eds.). *Progress in Communication Sciences*, 5: 45-71, 1984.

Q: An Interpretation of the Information Theoretical Q-measures. Pp. 63-67 in Robert Trapple, George Klir & Franz Pichler (Eds.). Progress in *Cybernetics and Systems Research Vol. VIII*. New York: Hemisphere, 1982. https://repository.upenn.edu/asc_papers/824

On the Identification of Latent Functions in Multi-Variate Data. Pp. 31-42 in Robert Trapple, George Klir & Franz Pichler (Eds.). *Progress in Cybernetics and Systems Research, Vol. VIII*. New York: Hemisphere, 1982. Regression Analysis Using Information Theory. Pp. 1007-1012. 1982 https://repository.upenn.edu/asc_papers/817

A Proposal for an Algorithm for Generating Loopless or Recursive Models of Multi-variate Data. Pp. 299- 304 in Len Troncale (Ed.). *A General Survey of Systems Methodology*. Louisville, KY: Society for General Systems Research, January 1982.
http://repository.upenn.edu/asc_papers/208

An algorithm for identifying structural models of multivariate data. *International Journal of General Systems* 7: 63-79, 1981.

Validity in Content Analysis. Chapter 3, pp. 69-112 in Ekkehard Mochmann (Ed.). *Computerstrategien für die Kommunikationsanalyse.* Frankfurt/New York: Campus, 1980.
http://repository.upenn.edu/asc_papers/291

Clustering. Chapter 9, pp. 259-308 in Peter R. Monge and Joseph N. Cappella (Eds.). *Multivariate Techniques in Communication Research.* New York: Academic Press, 1980. http://repository.upenn.edu/asc_papers/311

With Frederick Steier. Cybernetic Properties of Helping; the Organizational Level. Pp. 89-94 in Richard F. Ericson (Ed.). *Improving the Human Condition: Quality and Stability in Social Systems.* Louisville, KY: Society for General Systems Research, August 1979.
http://repository.upenn.edu/asc_papers/206.

On the Identification of Structures in Multi-variate Data by the Spectral Analysis of Relations. Pp. 82- 91 in Brian R. Gaines (Ed.). *General Systems Research: A Science, A Methodology, A Technology.* Louisville, KY: Society for General Systems Research, August 1979.
http://repository.upenn.edu/asc_papers/207

Viestinta ja jarjestelmateoria. Chapter 1.2, pp. 43-71 in Elja Erholm and Leif Aberg, (Eds.). *Viestinnan Virtauksia* (The flow of Communication). Helsinki, Finland: Otava Oy, 1978.

Information Systems, Theory and Research: An Overview. Pp. 149-171 in Brent D. Ruben, (Ed.). *Communication Yearbook I.* New Brunswick, NJ: Transactions, 1977.

The Systems Approach to Communication. Chapter 10, pp. 138-163 in Brent D. Ruben & John Y. Kim (Eds.). *General Systems Theory and Human Communication.* Rochelle Park, NJ: Hayden Book Co., 1975.

Information Theory. Chapter 17, pp. 351-389 in Gerhard J. Hanneman & William J. McEvan (Eds.). *Communication and Behavior.* Reading, MA: Addison-Wesley, 1975.

An Algorithm for simplifying the Representation of Complex Systems. Pp. 1693-1702 in John Rose (Ed.).*Advances in Cybernetics and Systems.* New York: Gorden & Breach, 1974.

With Marten Brouwer, Cedric C. Clark, Michael F. Eleey, and George Gerbner. Tabulation of Findings, Analytical Procedures, and Sampling of Programs, Appendices A, B, and C to George Gerbner. Violence in Television Drama: Trends and Symbolic Functions. Pp. 66-187 in George E. Comstock & Eli A. Rubinstein (Eds.). *Television and Social Behavior*; Reports and Papers, Volume I: A Technical Report to the Surgeon General's Scientific Advisory Committee on Television and Social Behavior. Washington, DC: U.S. Department of Health, Education, and Welfare Publication NSM 72-9057, 1972.

Bivariate Agreement Coefficients for Reliability of Data. Chapter 8, pp. 139-150 in Edgar R. Borgatta & George W. Bohrnstedt (Eds.). *Sociological Methodology 1970, Vol. 2*. San Francisco, CA: Jossey-Bass, Inc. 1970.

With Marten Brouwer, Cedric C. Clark, Michael F. Eleey, and George Gerbner. The Tele, pp. 311-339, and Content Analysis Procedures and Results. Pp. 519-591 in Robert K. Baker & Sandra J. Ball (Eds.). *Mass Media and Violence*, Vol. IX. A Report to the National Commission on the causes and prevention of violence. Washington, DC: U.S. Government Printing Office, November 1969. http://repository.upenn.edu/asc_papers/214

Models of Messages: Three Prototypes. Chapter 4, pp. 69-106 in George Gerbner, Ole R. Holsti, Klaus Krippendorff, William Paisley, & Philip J. Stone (Eds.). *The Analysis of Communication Content; Developments in Scientific Theories and Computer Techniques*. New York: John Wiley & Sons, 1969. http://repository.upenn.edu/asc_papers/282

Theories and Analytical Constructs (for Content Analysis), Introduction to Part 1. Pp. 3-16 in George Gerbner, Ole R. Holsti, Klaus Krippendorff, William Paisley, & Philip J. Stone (Eds.). *The Analysis of Communication Content: Developments in Scientific Theories and Computer Techniques*. New York: John Wiley & Sons, 1969.

Journal Articles
With Merzali Celikoglu, Ozge. Towards Ethnographies of Unimagined Possibilities: A New Paradigm for Human-centered Design Research. 2022 submitted.

A comment on "The Russia-Ukraine War and Its Systemic Solution". *Avances Sistémicos 5,* 3: 10-11, 2022.

A Quadrilogy for (Big) Data Reliabilities. *Communication Methods and Measures 15*, 3:165-189, 2021. https://doi.org/10.1080/19312458.2020.186 1592 A software for binary data and explanations (2021) is accessible at: https://www.asc.upenn.edu/quadrilogy

Book review of K. Krippendorff & N. Halabi (Eds.) *Discourses in Actions*. By Liqing Zhang. Journal of Language and Politics issn 1569-2159 | e-issn 1569-9862, Published 16 March, 2021 online: https://doi.org/10.1075/jlp.21013.zha

With Ozge Celikoglu Merzali, & Timur Ogut Sebnem. Inviting ethnographic conversations to inspire design: towards a design research method. *The Design Journal 23*, 1:133-152, 2019. https://doi.org/10.1080/14606925.2019.1693209 .

Designkutatás: Oximoron? Hungarian translation of "Design Research; An Oxymoron?" by P. Wunderlich. *Disegno, Journal of Design Culture IV*, 01-02: 72-87. 2019. https://doi.org/10.21096/disegno_2019_1-2kk

My scholarly life in cybernetics. *World Futures: The Journal of New Paradigm Research 75*, 1-2: 69-91, 2019, Jocelyn Chapman (Ed.). https://doi.org/10.1080/02604027.2019.1568803

Senior Communication Scholars' Advice to and Expectations of Young Researchers. A Dialogue, edited by Clement So. *Communication & Society 49:* 1-41, 2019. (In Chinese and English)

A discussion with Clement Y. K. So: The Changing Landscape of Content Analysis: Reflections on Social Construction of Reality and Beyond. *Communication & Society 47:* 1-27, 2019. (In Chinese and English). https://repository.upenn.edu/asc_papers/604

Socio-technological consequences of design discourse. Projetando socialilidades o discurso do design e seus impactos. An interview by Pamilla Vilas Boas Costa Ribeiro. *iDeia Design Magazinebook, 2:* 64- 71, 2018. (in Portuguese and English) https://repository.upenn.edu/asc_papers/603
http://ed2.revistaideia.com/project/magazine-book-volume-ii-2018/

Monologic versus Dialogic Distinctions of Selves. *Constructivist Foundations 13*, 1: 109-112, 2017.

Three Concepts to Retire. *Annals of the International Communication Association 41,* 1: 92-99, 2017. DOI: 10.1080/23808985.2017.1291281. https://repository.upenn.edu/asc_papers/629

Ozge Merzali Celikoglu; Sebnem Timur Ogut & Klaus Krippendorff. How do user stories inspire design? A study of cultural probes. *Design Issues 33,* 2: 84-98. 2017. https://repository.upenn.edu/asc_papers/511

Misunderstanding Reliability. Methodology, *(European Journal of Research Methods for the Behavioral and Social Sciences) 12* (4): 139-144, 2016. DOI: 10.1027/1614-2241/a000119; https://repository.upenn.edu/asc_papers/537

Rediseñar el diseño una invitacióón a un futuro responsible. *Infolio 5:* 1-21, 1-05-2016. (ISSN 2255-4564) http://infolio.es/articulos/krippendorff/krippendorf05.htm, http://infolio.es/articulos/krippendorff/redesign.pdf https://repository.upenn.edu/asc_papers/529

With Mathet, Yann; Bouvry, Stéphane & Widlöcher, Antoine. On the Reliability of Unitizing Textual Continua: Further Developments. *Quality & Quantity 50,* 6: 2347-2364, 2016. Online since 2015.9.15 at https://link.springer.com/article/10.1007/s11135-015-0266-1 also at https://www.researchgate.net/publication/272581846_On_the_Reliability_of_Unitizing_Continuous_Data

With Craggs, Richard. The Reliability of Multi-Valued Coding of Data. *Communication Methods and Measures 10,* 4: 181-198, 2016. DOI: 10.1080/19312458.2016.1228863.

With Barry Clemson. A Merger of Two Strategic (Ir)reconcilables, 1962-1980. *Cybernetics and Human Knowing 23,* 1: 10-18, 2016. CHK 23(1).book (chkjournal.com)

Groll, Sandra (Ed.). Traces and Hopes of Design Research: An Interview with Gui Bonsiepe, Klaus Krippendorff, Siegfried Maser, and René Spitz. *Design Issues 31,* 1: 18-31, 2015. https://repository.upenn.edu/asc_papers/509

Design centrado no ser humano: uma Necessidade cultural, G. Meirelles & L. Niemeyer (Tr.) of "Human- centered design: a cultural necessity" Paper presented at the IV Congresso Brasileiro de Pesquisa e Desenvolvimeto em Design. Feevale Centro Universitário, Nova Hamburgo: *Estudos em Design–Rio de Janeiro 8,* 3: 87-98, 2000. https://repository.upenn.edu/asc_papers/822

Design Principles. *Digital Art Criticism No 4:* 88-94, 2014. (Chinese translation of Klaus Krippendorff's New Design Principles, Chapter 3 in his (Ed.), Design in the Age of Information, A Report to the National Science Foundation (NSF). Raleigh, NC: Design Research Laboratory, School of Design, North Carolina State University, 1997).

Creating Identities. *Grid, 004:* 96-100, 2013. (Republication and translation into German of Section 4.4 of Klaus Krippendorff's (2006) *The Semantic Turn; A New foundation for Design*).

With Gabriela Trindade Perry (first author). On the reliability of identifying design moves in protocol analysis. *Design Studies 35,* 5: 612-635, 2013.

A dissenting view on so-called paradoxes of reliability coefficients. *Communication Yearbook 36:* Chapter 20, pp. 481-499 in C. T. Salmond, (Ed.). New York: Routledge, 2012. DOI:10.1080/23808985.2013.11679143.

Le discours et la matérialité de ses artefacts. *Communication & Languages 173:* 17-42, 2012/3. https://www.cairn.info/revue-communication-et-langages1-2012-3-page-17.htm

Human-centered design; A cultural necessity. Edited reprint of "A Trajectory of Artificiality and New Principles of Design for the Information Age" 1997. *Collection 3:* 33-40. 2011. Paris, France: Ecole Parsons à Paris.

Investigación en diseño, ¿un oxymoron? Traducción con fines exclusivamente académicos por: Alfredo Gutiérrez Borrero. (14 de julio de 2011) https://utadeo.academia.edu/AlfredoGuti%C3%A9rrez
Agreement and Information in the Reliability of Coding. *Communication Measures and Methods 5,* 2: 93- 112, 2011. http://repository.upenn.edu/asc_papers/278

Principles of design and a trajectory of artificiality. *Journal of Product Innovation Management 28,* 3: 411- 418, 2011. https://onlinelibrary.wiley.com/doi/full/10.1111/j.1540-5885.2011.00814.x

Conversation: Possibilities of its Repair and Descent into Discourse and Computation. *Constructivist Foundations 4,* 3: 135-147, 2009. http://repository.upenn.edu/asc_papers/134

Information of interactions in complex systems. *International Journal of General Systems* 38, 6: 669-680, 2009.
http://repository.upenn.edu/asc_papers/334

Social Organizations as Reconstitutable Networks of Conversation. *Cybernetics and Human Knowing* 15, 3- 4: 149-161, 2008.
http://repository.upenn.edu/asc_papers/135

Cybernetics's Reflexive Turns. *Cybernetics and Human Knowing* 15, 3-4: 173-184, 2008. http://repository.upenn.edu/asc_papers/136

Ross Ashby's Information Theory: A bit of History, Some Solutions to Problems, and What We Face Today. *International Journal of General Systems* 38, 2: 189-212, 2009. Correction of Figure 12, International Journal of General Systems 38, 6: 667-668, 2009.
http://repository.upenn.edu/asc_papers/237

Systematic and Random Disagreement and the Reliability of Nominal Data. *Communication Methods and Measures* 2, 4: 323-338, 2008. http://repository.upenn.edu/asc_papers/205

Towards a Radically Social Constructivism. *Constructivist Foundation* 3, 2: 91-94, 2008. http://repository.upenn.edu/asc_papers/133

The Cybernetics of Design and the Design of Cybernetics. *Kybernetes* 36, 9-10: 1381-1392, 2007. http://repository.upenn.edu/asc_papers/48/

An Exploration of Artificiality. *Artifact 1*, 1: 17-22, 2007 (paper version).
http://repository.upenn.edu/asc_papers/238

Andrew F. Hayes & Klaus Krippendorff: Answering the Call for a Standard Reliability Measure for Coding Data. *Communication Methods and Measures* 1, 1: 77-89, 2007. www.bwgriffin.com/gsu/courses/edur9131/content/coding_reliability_2007.pdf

The Dialogical Reality of Meaning; *The American Journal of Semiotics* 19, 1-4: 17-34, (actually 2006, nominally) 2003. http://repository.upenn.edu/asc_papers/51

Being Blind or Forgetting? *Research After All is Re-search; Aviso* 40: 8-9, 2005. http://repository.upenn.edu/asc_papers/38

Kommunikation als Überlebensfaktor in Unternehmen. Interview with Kerstin Richter in *Lernende Organisation 21:* 36-41, September/October 2004.

Die Folgen der Form von Kommunikationstheorien. Presentation at the Zentrum fur Medienkommunikation. Universitat Hamburg. *Aviso,* 37: 19, 2004.

Measuring the Reliability of Qualitative Text Analysis Data; *Quality and Quantity 38:* 787-800, 2004. http://repository.upenn.edu/asc_papers/42/

Reliability in Content Analysis: Some Common Misconceptions and Recommendations. *Human Communication Research 30,* 3: 411-433, 2004. http://repository.upenn.edu/asc_papers/242

Intrinsic Motivation and Human-centered Design; *Theoretical Issues in Ergonomics Science 5,* 1: 43-72, 2004. http://repository.upenn.edu/asc_papers/47

Recollections of Heinz von Foerster, a rhetorical genius. *Cybernetics & Human Knowing 10,* 3-4: 195-196, 2003. http://repository.upenn.edu/asc_papers/284

Rhetorische Geniestreiche. *Lernende Organisation, 11,* February: 59-60, 2003.

Afterword (to an issue devoted to the work of Francisco J. Varela). *Cybernetics & Human Knowing 9,* 2: 95-96, 2002. http://repository.upenn.edu/asc_papers/308

Design centrado no ser humano: uma necessidade cultural. *Revista Estudos em Design, Rio de Janeiro 8,* 3: 87-98, 2000. http://periodicos.anhembi.br/arquivos/Hemeroteca/Periodicos_MO/Estudos_em_Design/107170.pdf

De la construction des gens dans l'enquête sociale. *Reviue europédes sciences socials,* Tome XXXVII (114): 37-55, 1999. http://repository.upenn.edu/asc_papers/285

Beyond Coherence. *Management Communication Quarterly 13,* 1: 135-145, 1999. http://repository.upenn.edu/asc_papers/240

Wenn ich einen Stuhl sehe - sehe ich dann wirklich nur ein Zeichen? When I See a Chair - Must I See a Sign of It? *formdiskurs 5,* 2: 98-107, 1998. http://repository.upenn.edu/asc_papers/39

With Nelda Samarel and Jacqueline Fawcett: Women's perceptions of group support and adaptation to breast cancer. *Journal of Advanced Nursing 28,* 6: 1259-1268, 1998. http://repository.upenn.edu/asc_papers/309.

A Second-order Cybernetics of Otherness. *Systems Research 13,* 3: 311-328, 1996. http://repository.upenn.edu/asc_papers/80

Undoing Power. *Critical Studies in Mass Communication 12,* 2: 101-132, 1995. http://repository.upenn.edu/asc_papers/82

Major Metaphors of Communication and some Constructivist Reflections on their Use. *Cybernetics & Human Knowing 2,* 1: 3-25, 1993. http://repository.upenn.edu/asc_papers/84

The Past of Communication's Hoped-For Future. *Journal of Communication 43,* 3: 34-44, 1993. http://repository.upenn.edu/asc_papers/532

Where Meanings Escape Functions, with Reinhart Butter. *Design Management Journal 4,* 2: 30-37, 1993. http://repository.upenn.edu/asc_papers/332

Conversation or Intellectual Imperialism in Comparing Communication (Theories). *Communication Theory 3,* 3: 252-266, 1993. http://repository.upenn.edu/asc_papers/257
Information, Information Society, and Some Marxian Propositions. *Information and Behavior 5:* 487-521, 1992. http://repository.upenn.edu/asc_papers/216.

The Power of Communication and the Communication of Power; Toward an Emancipatory Theory of Communication. *Communication 12:* 175-196, 1989 (published 1991).

Imaging, Computing and Designing Minds. *Design Management Journal 2,* 1: 29-36, 1991. http://repository.upenn.edu/asc_papers/234.

Eine häretische Kommunikation über Kommunikation über Kommunikation über Realität. *Delfin 13,* 2: 52- 67, January, 1990.
http://repository.upenn.edu/asc_papers/235

The Language of Objects, with Seppo Väkevä. *Blueprint 52,* June 1989.
http://repository.upenn.edu/asc_papers/215

Design muss Sinn machen; zu einer neuen Design Theorie. Hochschule für Gestaltung Offenbach's *hfg- forum 14:* 24-30, November, 1989.
http://repository.upenn.edu/asc_papers/252

"On the Essential Contexts of Artifacts" or on the Proposition that "Design is Making Sense (of Things)." *Design Issues 5,* 2: 9-39, 1989.
http://www.jstor.org/pss/1511512

Association, Agreement, and Equity. *Quality and Quantity 21:* 109-123, 1987.

Japanese translation of Exploring the Symbolic Qualities of Form, with Reinhart Butter. *Industrial Design 139-140:* 10-13, 1987.
http://repository.upenn.edu/asc_papers/40

With Michael Eleey, Monitoring a Group's Symbolic Environment. *Public Relations Review 12,* 1: 13-36, 1986.

Information, Information Society and Some Marxian Propositions (Shortened version of http://repository.upenn.edu/asc_papers/216). *Informatologia Yugoslavica 17,* 1-2: 7-38, 1985.

Comments on Richard Buchanan's "Declaration by Design." *Design Issues 2,* 2: 71-72, 1985. http://repository.upenn.edu/asc_papers/217
Communication from a Cybernetic Perspective. *Informatologia Yugoslavica 16,* 1&2: 51-78, 1985.
http://repository.upenn.edu/asc_papers/218

Die Produkt-Semantik öffnet die Türen zu einem neuen Bewusstsein im Design. *Form 108-109:* 14-16, 1984-85.
http://repository.upenn.edu/asc_papers/236

Fred Hermann: Experimente in Sachen Semantik. Form 108-109, 17-19, 1984-85. http://repository.upenn.edu/asc_papers/41

Exploring the Symbolic Qualities of Form, with Reinhart Butter. *Innovations 3*, 2: 4-9, 1984. http://repository.upenn.edu/asc_papers/40

An Epistemological Foundation for Communication. *Journal of Communication 34,* 3: 21-36, 1984. https://repository.upenn.edu/asc_papers/538

An Algorithm for Identifying Structural Models of Multi-variate Data. *International Journal of Systems Science 7:* 63-79, 1981.

On the Cybernetics of Time, *Systemsletter 7,* 1: 1-2, 1978. http://repository.upenn.edu/asc_papers/228

Reliability of Binary Attribute Data. With comments by Joseph L Fleiss. *Biometrics 34,* 1: 142-144, 1978. http://www.jstor.org/pss/2529602

Some Principles of Information Storage and Retrieval in Society. *General Systems 20:* 15-35, 1975. http://repository.upenn.edu/asc_papers/229
Reprinted in Communications 4, 1: 5-34, & 4,2: 141-156, 1978.

Conclusions from the ASC Conference on Communication and Control in Social Processes, October 31- November 2, 1974 at the University of Pennsylvania. *Kybernetes 4:* 188-189, 1975; Cybernetics Forum 7, 1: 22-23, 1975. https://repository.upenn.edu/asc_papers/539

Adding Large Numbers by Computer. *Journal of Cybernetics 3,* 3: 13-14, 1973.

A Calculus for Disagreements: A Categorial Equivalence to Variance Analysis. *General Systems 16:* 222- 235, 1971. http://repository.upenn.edu/asc_papers/219
Communication and the Genesis of Structure. *General Systems 16:* 171-185, 1971. http://repository.upenn.edu/asc_papers/225

Reliability of Recording Instructions: Multivariate Agreement for Nominal Data. *Behavior Science 16:* 222- 235, 1971.

The Expression of Values in Political Documents. *Journalism Quarterly 47:* 510-518, 1970. https://repository.upenn.edu/asc_papers/530

On Generating Data in Communication Research. *Journal of Communication 20:* 241-269, 1970.
http://repository.upenn.edu/asc_papers/273

Estimating the Reliability, Systematic Error and Random Error of Interval Data. *Educational and Psychological Measurement 30:* 61-70, 1970.

Values, Modes and Domains of Inquiry into Communication. *Journal of Communication 19:* 105-133, 1969.

Produktgestalter Kontra Konstrukteur. *Output 5+6:* 18-21, 1961.
http://repository.upenn.edu/asc_papers/299

der komnunikative aspekt der produktgestaltung: gegenstände als zeichen und symbole. Presentation at the Hochschule für Gestaltung Ulm, January 2, 1961. http://repository.upenn.edu/asc_papers/808

Publications in Informal Conference Proceedings

A Critical Cybernetics. Paper presented at the American Society for Cybernetics (ICA) track at the meeting of the International Society for the Systems Sciences (ISSS), July 7–13, 2021. ASC Speaker Series #3 - Towards a Critical Cybernetics by Klaus Krippendorff - YouTube

Agency, algorithms, a new form of oppression and how cyberneticians might respond. Keynote to the American Society for Cybernetic (ASC) meeting in Montreal, Canada, 2019.06.22-27.

Social Implications of Three Models of Design. Keynote address to an international conference titled "Design for a Billion" hosted by the Indian Institute of Technology, Gandhinagar, November 7-9, 2014.

A Conversation with Ken Friedman on the Challenges that Digital Media Present to Design Discourse, Education, and Practice. On the occasion of the 20th anniversary celebration of the Media Lab at Aalto University in Helsinki, September 25, 2014.

A Future for Cybernetics. Keynote address to the 50th anniversary meeting of the American Society for Cybernetics at the George Washington University in Washington, DC, August 3-9, 2014.

Languaging Reality; Dialogue and Interaction. Keynote address to a conference on *"Language and Interaction"* February 6-8, 2014 in Amsterdam, organized by the international Interaction Design Conference (IxDA). http://vimeo.com/album/2488675/video/86240674

Designing Differences that Make a Difference. Keynote address to a conference titled; *"The Relationships between Design and Society"* held December 13, 2013 at the University of Art and Design, Offenbach/Main, Germany.

Krippendorff en la Tadeo [Españiol] (2011). Por: Alfredo Gutiérrez Borrero. https://www.academia.edu/16989307/Krippendorff_en_la_Tadeo_Espa%C3%B1ol_2011_

Krippendorff's Alpha. Pp.669-673 in *The SAGE Encyclopedia of Research Design*. Neil Salkind (Ed.). Thousand Oaks, CA.: SAGE Publications. 2010.

Reconciling Radical Constructivism with Social Organizations as Networks of Conversations and Stakeholders. Prepared for presentation but not delivered at the 2008 Conference of the American Society of Cybernetics, May 11-15, Urbana, IL. http://www.asc-cybernetics.org/2008/Krippendorff.htm; https://repository.upenn.edu/asc_papers/528

The Diversity of Meanings of Cultural Artifacts and Human-Centered Design. Paper prepared for the DeSForM 2008 Conference, November 6-7, 2008, at the Hochschule für Gestaltung Offenbach, University of Frankfurt/Main.

Information and Cyberspace: Re-embodying Information Theory. Presentation on the occasion of receiving the Norbert Wiener/Hermann Schmidt Prize by the German Society for Cybernetics and the German Society for Pedagogy and Information, at the University of Vienna, 2004. http://www.gpi-online.de/upload/PDFs/EU-Media/_Krippendorf-ViennaInfCyberspace-EN.pdf

Product Semantics: A Brief Sketch. *4th Congresso Brasileiro de Pesquisa & Desenvolimento em Design*. Novo Hamburgo: Feevale Centro Universitário, October 29 - November 1, 2000.

Human-centered Design; A Cultural Imperative. *4th Congresso Brasileiro de Pesquisa & Desenvolimento em Design*. Novo Hamburgo: Feevale Centro Universitário, October 29 - November 1, 2000.

Design Discourse; A Way to Redesign Design. Keynote address to the Society for Science of Design Studies. Tokyo, Japan: December 6, 1998, in press. http://repository.upenn.edu/asc_papers/227

On Human-Centeredness in Design. Proceedings of the International workshop on Semantics in Design and the Linguistic Nature of Things, Munich, Germany, February 18-20, 1998.
http://semantics-in-design.hfg- gmuend.de

Stakeholder Theory. Proceedings of the International workshop on Semantics in Design and the Linguistic Nature of Things, Munich, Germany, February 18-20, 1998.
http://repository.upenn.edu/asc_papers/230

Human-Centeredness; A Paradigm Shift Invoked by the Emerging Cyberspaces. Keynote at a symposium on Connected Intelligence; *Human Beings in Information Systems* at the Zentrum für Kunst und Medientechnologie, Karlsruhe, Germany, October 27-28, 1997. http://repository.upenn.edu/asc_papers/85

On the Embodiment of Recursive Communication (Theory). Pp. 6-7 in Proceedings of the American Society for Cybernetics meeting on *Cybernetics and Circularity in Honor of Heinz von Foerster*, at the University of Illinois at in Chicago, May 16, 1995. https://repository.upenn.edu/asc_papers/826

Design muss Sinn machen; zu einer neuen Design Theorie. Paper presented at the International Forum für Gestaltung, Ulm, Germany, September 2-4, 1988. Proceedings published 1989. http://repository.upenn.edu/asc_papers/252

A Proposal for an Algorithm for Generating Loopless or Recursive Models of Multi-variate Data. Pp. 299- 304 in Len Troncale (Ed.), in *A General Survey of Systems Methodology*. Louisville, KY: Society for General Systems Research, January 1982.
http://repository.upenn.edu/asc_papers/208

Q: An Interpretation of the Information Theoretical Q-measures. Fifth European Meeting for Cybernetics and Systems Research, Vienna, April 1980. A software, written in Fortran, to compute the quantities developed here is available at
http://www.leydesdorff.net/software/krippendorff/index.htm.

On Systems Thinking. Pp. 13-21 in Paul Broholm and Nic van Dijk (Eds.). *Systems Thinking and Social Science,* Proceedings of a Symposium held at the Inter-universitaire Interfaculteit Bedrijfskunde. Delft. The Netherlands, November 15, 1979.
https://repository.upenn.edu/asc_papers/815

With Frederick Steier. Cybernetic Properties of Helping; the Organizational Level. Conference of the Society for General Systems Research: *Improving the Human Condition: Quality and Stability in Social Systems.* London, England, August 1979.
http://repository.upenn.edu/asc_papers/206

Book Reviews

The Construction of Social Reality, by John R. Searle. New York: The Free Press, 1995. Cybernetics & Human Knowing 3, 4: 23-26, 1996. http://repository.upenn.edu/asc_papers/232 also published in Communication Theory 7, 1: 81-85, 1997.

Ecological Communication, by Niklas Luhmann. Chicago. IL: University of Chicago Press, 1989. *Journal of Communication 41,* 1: 136-140, 1991.
https://repository.upenn.edu/asc_papers/527

Angels Fear: Toward an Epistemology of the Sacred, by Gregory Bateson and Mary Catherine Bateson. New York: MacMillan, 1987. *Journal of Communication 38,* 3: 167-171, 1988. https://repository.upenn.edu/asc_papers/536 Republished in Continuing the Conversation 11: 1-2, Winter 1987.

The Dream of Reality: Heinz von Foerster's Constructivism, by Lynn Segal. New York & London: Norton, 1986. *Journal of Communication 37,* 2: 155-158, 1987. https://repository.upenn.edu/asc_papers/534

Basic Content Analysis, by Robert P. Weber. Beverly Hills, CA: Sage Publications, 1985. *Journal of the American Statistical Association 82*: 354-355, 1987. https://repository.upenn.edu/asc_papers/540

Interact with complexity. Book review of *The Sciences and Praxis of Complexity.* New York: U.N. University, 1985. *Journal of Communication 36,* 3: 180-183, 1986.

Self-Organization and Management of Social Systems: Insights, Promises, Doubts and Questions, by H. Ulrich and G.J.B. Probst (Eds.). Berlin: Springer 1984. *European Journal of Operational Research* 27: 253- 254, 1986.
https://repository.upenn.edu/asc_papers/531

System and Structure: Essays in Communication and Exchange, by Anthony Wilden. London: Travistock Publications, 1972. *Contemporary Sociology* 5, 3: 291-292, 1976.

Gewalt im Fernsehen: Literaturbericht über Medienwirkungs-Forschung, by Helga Kellner and Imme Horn, Mainz, Germany: Universitäts-Druckerei, 1971. Journal of Communication 24, 1: 137, 1974.
https://repository.upenn.edu/asc_papers/542

Content Analysis: A Technique for Systematic Inferences from Communications, by Thomas F. Carney. Winnipeg: University of Manitoba Press, 1972. *Public Opinion Quarterly* 38, 1: 155-157, Spring 1974.
https://repository.upenn.edu/asc_papers/535

Crime and Information Theory, by M.A.P. Willmer. Edinburgh and Chicago: Edinburgh University Press and Aldine Publishing Company, 1970. *Journal of Communication 21,* 3: 280-294, 1971.

Cybernetic Principles of Learning and Educational Design, by Karl U. Smith and Margaret Foltz Smith, New York: Holt, Rinehart and Winston, Inc., 1966. *AV Communication Review 15,* 2: 216-218, 1967.

Wff'n Proof, The Game of Modern Logic, by Layman E. Allen. New Haven, Conn.: Box 71, 1962. Equations, The Game of Creative Mathematics, by Layman E. Allen. New Haven CT: Box 71, 1963. *AV Communication Review 14,* 1: 86-87, 1965.

Psychologie der Massenkommunikation: Theorie und Systematik, by Gerhard Maletzke. Hamburg: Hans Bredow Institut, 1963. *Journalism Quarterly* 41: 592-594, 1964.

Umfragen in der Massengesellschaft: Einführung in die Methoden der Demoskopie, by Elisabeth Noelle, Reinbeck bei Hamburg: Rowohlt, 1963. *AV Communication Review 12,* 4: 468-470, 1964.

On Film as Film. Film und Philosophie, Ein Essai, by Gilbert Cohen-Seat. Gütersloh, Germany: C. Bertelsmann Verlag, 1962. *Film und*

Verkündung, Probleme des religiösen Films, by Gerd Albrecht. Gütersloh: C. Bertelsmann Verlag, 1962. *Die Deutsche Filmmusik von den Anfängen bis 1956.* by Hans Alex Thomas. Gütersloh: C. Bertelsmann Verlag, 1962. *AV Communication Review 11,* 6: 297-299, 1963.

Theorie der Massenmedien: Presse, Film, Rundfunk, by Erich Feldmann. München-Basel: Ernst Reinhardt Verlag 1962. *AV Communication Review 11,* 3: 64-65, 1963.

Research Reports and Proposals

Replacement of Section 12.4 in Klaus Krippendorff. Content Analysis; An Introduction to Its Methodology.3rd Edition. Thousand Oaks, CA: Sage Publications, 2013. To be introduced into its 2nd printing Originally posted 2014.4.12, revised 2015.9.23 http://web.asc.upenn.edu/usr/krippendorff/m- Replacement%20of%20section%2012.4%20on%20unitizing%20continua%20in%20CA,%203rd%20ed.pdf

Bootstrapping Distributions for Krippendorff's Alpha Substantially improved 2016 http://www.asc.upenn.edu/boot.c-Alpha

Algorithm for bootstrapping a distribution of $_c a$, 2006 (mimeo) revised 2013 http://www.asc.upenn.edu/usr/krippendorff/m-BootstrappingRevised.pdf

Computing Krippendorff's Alpha-Reliability, 2007 (mimeo) revised 2011 http://repository.upenn.edu/asc_papers/43

Propositions of Human-centeredness; an Epistemology for Design. Paper prepared for a conference on a Ph.D. in Design

A Content Analysis of Bias in *Consumer Reports* on Automobiles. A Report of Research. Philadelphia: The Annenberg School of Communications, University of Pennsylvania, 1982 (mimeo). http://repository.upenn.edu/asc_papers/220

Proof for and illustration of an algorithm that distinguishes structural models with loops from those without loops. Philadelphia: The Annenberg School of Communications, University of Pennsylvania, 1981 (mimeo).

Development and Aid; A Study of Self-Organization in Bangladesh Villages. A Proposal for Research. Philadelphia: The Annenberg School of Communications, University of Pennsylvania, 1978 (mimeo).

A Spectral Analysis of Relations. Philadelphia: The Annenberg School of Communication, University of Pennsylvania, 1976 (mimeo). http://repository.upenn.edu/asc_papers/223

A Method for the Strong Associative Clustering of 2m Data. Philadelphia: The Annenberg School of Communications, University of Pennsylvania, 1975 (mimeo). http://repository.upenn.edu/asc_papers/221

With Mike Eleey. A System for the Continual Monitoring of National Publicity for PBS Programming. Report of a Pilot Study. The Public Broadcasting Service, Washington DC, March 5, 1973.

Some Patterns in Violent Interaction on Television. A preliminary report, Philadelphia: The Annenberg School of Communications, University of Pennsylvania, 1969 (mimeo).

Computer Programs for Multivariate Classification in Content Analysis. A research Proposal submitted to the National Science Foundation. Philadelphia: The Annenberg School of Communications, University of Pennsylvania, 1969 (mimeo).

Suggested Domain and Structure of a Ph.D. Program in Social Communication Science. Philadelphia: The Annenberg School of Communications, University of Pennsylvania, 1965 (mimeo.). http://repository.upenn.edu/asc_papers/231

An Outline for BATIC: A Teaching Device for Demonstration of and Experimentation with Basic Automata Theory In Cybernetics and in Communications. Philadelphia: The Annenberg School of Communications, University of Pennsylvania, 1964 (mimeo).

First Notes on Simulating Future-Directed Behavior of Very Large Social Systems on the Basis of the Message Content Circulating Within those Systems. Urbana, IL: Institute of Communications Research, University of Illinois, 1964 (mimeo).

Einfluß der Farbe auf die Erkennbarkeit und Auffälligkeit von Objekten. With Mervyn W. Perrine and Klaus Wegner. Ulm, Germany: Hochschule für Gestaltung, Research Center for Visual Perception, Technical Report 3, 1961. http://repository.upenn.edu/asc_papers/310

Computer Programs and Instructions

A Quadrilogy of Big Binary Data Reliabilities. Plus users' instructions and mathematical explanations 2021: https://www.asc.upenn.edu/quadrilogy

CONSTRUCT, a computer program for confirmatory analysis of structural models for qualitative data using information theory. Philadelphia: The Annenberg School of Communications, University of Pennsylvania, 1988.

A Computer Program for Strong Associative Clustering of 2m. Data. Philadelphia: The Annenberg School of Communications, University of Pennsylvania, 1975 (mimeo).

A Computer Program for Agreement Analysis of Reliability Data (Version 4b), User's Manual. Philadelphia: The Annenberg School of Communications, University of Pennsylvania, July 1973 (mimeo).

A Computer Program for Contingency Analysis, User's Manual. Philadelphia: The Annenberg School of Communications, University of Pennsylvania, 1970 (mimeo).

A Computer Program for Analyzing Semantic Information Content of Symbols, User's Manual. Philadelphia: The Annenberg School of Communication, University of Pennsylvania, 1970 (mimeo).

A Computer Program for Analyzing Multivariate Agreements, User's Manual. Philadelphia: The Annenberg School of Communications, University of Pennsylvania, 1968 (mimeo), Version 2 (1970), version 3 (1973).

A Computer Program for Assessing Agreements Among Many Judges When Data Are Nominal-Scale- Recorded. Philadelphia: The Annenberg School of Communications, University of Pennsylvania, 1968.

Other Papers, Presentations, and Work in Progress

Four theories of using language. Online presentation to the Club of Remy. November 10, 2021. https://www.youtube.com/watch?v=jYnSbNobc3Y

From uncritical design to critical examinations of its systemic consequences. Keynote address to RSD10 conference in Delft, NL, on relating systems thinking to design, November 4, 2021. https://rsdsymposium.org/professor-dr-klaus-krippendorff/

A Critical Cybernetics. Keynote paper presented at the American Society for Cybernetics (ICA) track during the online meeting of the International Society for the Systems Sciences (ISSS), July 7–13, 2021.

Problems have no problem; Who does? Online presentation to the Club of Remy. May 5, 2021. https://www.youtube.com/watch?v=Y9BqQ1tIzSk

Seven complexities of social organizations. Online discussion at the Club of Remy. April 7, 2021. https://www.youtube.com/watch?v=AUrBH75gQSs

Conversations and their decay into other forms of communication. Online presentation to the Club of Remy. March 17, 2021. https://www.youtube.com/watch?v=c4pgxj8krTs
Towards a critical cybernetics. Online presentation to the Club of Remy. February 3, 2021. https://www.youtube.com/watch?v=VnF8_enkWKM

Escaping Entrapments in Uni-verses. Paper presented at a conference "What Is Universe", University of Oregon, Portland OR, April 21, 2018. An Ecology of Artifacts in Language - YouTube

Agency and Discourse; Who is Talking and Acting – not What. Aubrey Fisher Memorial Lecture delivered at the Department of Communication, The University of Utah, Salt Lake City, October 19, 2017.

Three Models of Design – Notes for a keynote address delivered at a conference entitled: *Design for a Billion* at the Indian Institute of Technology, Gandhinagar, November 7-8, 2014.

Research vs. Design. Paper presentation at the Bauhaus-Universität Weimar, Germany, 2013.

From Conversation to Discourse. Presentation at USC's Annenberg School for Communication. Los Angeles, October 10, 2011.

Shifting Epistemology from Complexity to Reflexivity. Paper presented at the 2nd conference of the World Complexity Science Academy, Palermo, Italy, September 26-27, 2011.

Discourse and its Artifacts; Technology and Language Use. Presentation at the International Communication Association, Singapore, 2010.

The Diversity of Meanings of Everyday Artifacts and Human-Centered Design. Presented at the DeSForM Conference in Offenbach, November 6-7, 2008.

Language in the Constitution of Social Systems. Presentation at the International Society for the Systems Sciences (ISSS), Sonoma, 2006. Recollections for the Gerbner-Memorial on 2006.4.8

Second-order Cybernetics, A Conversation that Reflects on Itself. Philadelphia: The Annenberg School for Communication, University of Pennsylvania, 2000.

Writing: Monologue, Dialogue, and Ecological Narrative. Paper presented to the conference of Writing Across the Curriculum (WAC). Ithaca, NY: Cornell University, June 3-6, 1999. For publication in Jonathan Monroe (Ed.), *Virtual Fields: Academic Discourse and Post-Disciplinary Cultures* (Publication project abandoned).

Doing Cybernetics. Presentation to a conference of the American Society for Cybernetics meeting on February 19, 1999 in Urbana-Champaign. Design Discourse: A Medium for Redesigning Design. Presentation to the Society for the Science of Design Studies, 1998.12.6, Tokyo, Japan. Written 1999.6.1. http://ssdsj.net/eng/index.html

A Paradigm Shift Invoked by the Emerging Cyberspaces. Paper presented to a conference on "Connected Intelligence; Humans in Information Systems" at the Center for Art and Media, Karlsruhe, Germany, October 28-30, 1997. Also discussed at the conference on Design, Planning and Human Understanding of the American Society for Cybernetics, April 2-5, 1998, Santa Cruz, CA.

The Social Reality of Meaning. Paper presented at a workshop on *The Meaning of Things,* March 17, 1996, Cooper-Hewitt, National Design Museum, Smithsonian Institution, New York.

Arguing in support of the proposition: *Resolved that "Knowledge about Communication Can Only Be Known By the Knower,"* made during the Information Systems Debate on 1996.5.24 at the ICA Conference in Chicago IL. http://repository.upenn.edu/asc_papers/286

The Semantic Turn; An Introduction to Product Semantics with Reference to Ulm. Principal paper presented to a conference convened for this purpose on December 3-4, 1994, at the Club off Ulm, Germany, Edited April 25, 1995.

The Principle of Reflexivity. Paper Presented at the ICA Conference in Washington DC, May 27-31, 1993.

Recent Developments in Reliability Analysis. Paper presented at the ICA Conference in Miami FL, May 21-25, 1992. http://repository.upenn.edu/asc_papers/44/

Disagreement and Reliability. Philadelphia: The Annenberg School for Communication, University of Pennsylvania, October 10, 1991 (mimeo).

Steppingstones Towards A Constructivist Epistemology for Mass Communication. Keynote address for a conference on Theories of Public Communication by the Deutsche Gesellschaft für Publizistik und Kommunikationswissenschaft, Bamberg, Germany, May 8-10, 1991. http://repository.upenn.edu/asc_papers/255

Information, In-formation and in Formation in Theory and Practice. Philadelphia: The Annenberg School for Communication, mimeo. Requested for publication, 1990.

On Reflexivity in Human Communication. Paper presented at the 10th Temple Conference on Discourse Analysis, March 16-18, 1989. Philadelphia: The Annenberg School for Communication, University of Pennsylvania, 1989 (mimeo). http://repository.upenn.edu/asc_papers/253

Receptions

"Das Schicksal (...) entscheidet sich in der Sprache" (The Fate (of...) is Decided in Language)" An extensive review of the German translation of *The Semantic Turn, a new Foundation for Design (Die semantische Wende, eine neue Grundlage für das Design)* in "Sprache für die Form, 4, 2014." http://www.designrhetorik.de/?page_id=4042.

Review of *Die semantische Wende* (German translation of *The Semantic Turn, a new Foundation for Design*) by Joachim Kobus http://www.designersbusiness.de/info/literatur/klaus-krippendorff. Blog: Designers Business. August 2013.

"Ästhetik und Semantik, Zwei Modelle." A comparison of Klaus Krippendorff's and Holger van den Bohm's theories of aesthetics and meaning by Felicidad Romero-Tejedor in: *"Öffnungszeiten, Papiere zur Designwissenschaft 27,* 39-51, 2013. http://www.uni-kassel.de/upress/online/OpenAccess/1613-5881_002.OpenAccess.pdf

Review of *The Semantic Turn; A New Foundation for Design* by Klaus Krippendorff. Reviewed by Pelle Ehn, Artifact 1 (1): 59-63. http://apptrevete.com/enfasis/imagenes/krippendorf_resumenlibro.pdf

Review of *The Semantic Turn; A New Foundation for Design* by Klaus Krippendorff. Reviewed by Austin Henderson. *Interactions* 13 (6): 56-59, 2006. http://dl.acm.org/citation.cfm?doid=1167948.1167988

Towards a Cybernetics of (Mass-Media) Institutions. Sari Thomas and Nancy Signorielli (Eds.). *Essays in Honor of George Gerbner,* proposed but not completed. http://repository.upenn.edu/asc_papers/251

On Poppings Agreement Indices. Philadelphia: The Annenberg School of Communications, University of Pennsylvania, 1988 (mimeo).

On Constructing People in Social Inquiry. Philadelphia: The Annenberg School of Communications, University of Pennsylvania, 1986 (mimeo).

Communication from a Cybernetic Perspective, East and West? Philadelphia: The Annenberg School of Communications, University of Pennsylvania, 1982 (mimeo).

Review of Communication and Control in Society, Klaus Krippendorff (Ed.) by Maria Novaskowska in the Polish Journal Prakseologia, May 1980.

The Model as a Communication Channel; A Quantitative Approach. Philadelphia: The Annenberg School of Communications, University of Pennsylvania, 1978 (mimeo).

A Spectral Analysis of Relations, Further Developments. Philadelphia: The Annenberg School of Communications, University of Pennsylvania, 1978 (mimeo). http://repository.upenn.edu/asc_papers/222

Reliability, The Case of Binary Attributes. Philadelphia: The Annenberg School of Communications, University of Pennsylvania, 1978 (mimeo).

Validity in Content Analysis. Philadelphia: The Annenberg School of Communications, University of Pennsylvania, 1977 (mimeo).

A Non-parametric Test of the Significance of Difference Between One and a Sample of Partitions of the Same Level. Philadelphia: The Annenberg School of Communications, University of Pennsylvania, 1973 (mimeo).

The Recording Process. Philadelphia: The Annenberg School of Communications, University of Pennsylvania, 1972 (mimeo).

What's Wrong with Content Analysis: A Methodological Critique. Paper presented to the Communication Theory and Methodology Division of the AEJ Annual Conference, Berkeley, CA, August 1969.
Philadelphia: The Annenberg School of Communications, University of Pennsylvania, 1969 (mimeo).

The Structure of an Algorithm for Identifying Values Expressed in Written Text. Philadelphia: The Annenberg School of Communications, University of Pennsylvania, 1965 (mimeo).